SACRAMENTO, D.C.

A Political Lampoon

BILL MILLER

Erin Press, Inc.

The people and events in this book are fictitious and fabrications.

Editing by Russell Fuller
Production by Bookman Productions
Jacket design by Stephen Osborn

Library of Congress Cataloging-in-Publication Data

Miller, Bill, 1938–
     Sacramento, D.C. :   a novel / by Bill Miller
        p.   cm.
     ISBN 0-929473-00-0
     I. Title
     PS3563.I3746S23 1989
     813' .54--dc19   88-30886
                                                            CIP

Printed in the United States of America

To Bob, George, and Vance

DEPARTMENT OF COMMERCE
UNITED STATES OF AMERICA

Sacramento
(sack-rah-men-toe)

According to *Webster's Third New International Dictionary* (unabridged), *Sacramento* is the name of the capital city of the state of California. Also listed under *sacramento* are *sacramento cat*, *sacramento perch*, *sacramento pike*, *sacramento salmon*, *sacramento sturgeon*, and *sacramento sucker*. However, none of these definitions appear to be directly related, and they reveal nothing about the city itself. The city's main point of interest seems to be a residence located east of the capitol grounds, which was the temporary home of a former California governor and future president of the United States, Ronald Wilson Reagan. Reagan moved to this residence when his wife, Nancy, declared the official governor's mansion a fire trap.

The metropolitan area surrounding the city is quite productive with rich farm land, small business, and light industry. But the city itself is inhabited primarily by transient politicians and their support staffs, including lobbyists, most of whom come from southern California. Although *all* indicators point to a nonproductive entity, the city appears to be quite well off financially, deriving most of its income, directly and indirectly, from the state treasury. The city at one time boasted of a locally produced and nationally distributed tomato juice bearing its name—alleged to go "plop-plop-plop" when poured from its container—but Sacramento brand tomato juice went out of business many years ago.

It appears that Sacramento is a government town, much like Washington, D.C., but on a smaller scale in terms of population and counterproductivity, with a relatively insignificant drain on the gross national product. As long as the city remains within its present boundaries, it poses no threat to the economy of the state of California or the United States of America.

(From an undated report found in the archives of the United States Department of Commerce.)

CHAPTER 1

IT WAS ONE OF those days. The kind of day that people talk about years later, remembering not the year but the day and what a wonderful time it was. The temperature was a perfect 78 degrees, and the air was moving a little less than a breeze, just enough to stir the new green leaves on the trees ever so slightly. The vernal grasses sprouting from the moist, warm earth reflected bright green in the late morning sun. The foothills to the northeast of Sacramento appeared to be covered with astroturf and the oak trees imported from Disneyland. It was the first spring of heavy rains after a three-year drought, and the California flora and fauna seemed truly born again.

The pandemic zephyr spread across the foothills and into the valley, rendering all but a very few inoculable. On the playgrounds rosy-cheeked little girls sat cross-legged on benches and pulled their skirt hems down over their knees, twittering and giggling as young boys danced and paraded before them. Young maidens locked themselves in their rooms and cautiously refused dates with their boyfriends or fiancés. Teenage boys, glassy-eyed and on rubbery legs, emerged from hiding places. Dallying husbands were late for work. Mrs. Olsen, several times a grandmother, spiked her husband's morning coffee with a double shot of Geritol and served it to him in bed. It was one of those days!

About twenty-five miles from the city center lay the vast, palatial Baal estate, where young J.J. Baal was thoroughly enjoying the effects of spring fever as he and his raven-haired, brown-eyed, olive-complected companion sat in a lawn swing, holding hands and kissing. Like any other seventeen-year-old engaged in his first major conquest, J.J. was in the moment and making the most of it. The thought of following family tradition and entering politics was the farthest thing from his mind, and just now no one in California would have guessed that in twenty-four years J.J. would be seeking his second term as governor, with aspirations to be president.

J.J. was christened Harry Hamilton Baal III, but from the time he drew his first breath, he was called Junior-Junior, later simply J.J. His father, U.S. Senator Harry Hamilton Baal, Jr., protested from the beginning, fearing that young Harry would lose the family name identification that he would need to launch his future political career. But his mother, Daphne Cole-Baal, a relocated belle from Mobile, Alabama, won out, and J.J. he became. "At least he won't be called Bubba," said the senator sarcastically, lamenting in defeat.

J.J. was not born with a silver spoon in his mouth but was certainly fed with one. The family wealth was such that the last member of the Baal family to hold legitimate employment was J.J.'s great-great-grandfather, and he was a part-time horse thief. Abraham Swanson Baal worked as a groom on a horse ranch and, over a period of years, stole and sold several expensive horses to help build his bankroll. Abraham was never caught, but two innocent men were convicted and hung for two of the thefts. In each case Abraham received a sizable reward for capturing the thief. His only offspring, Swanson Hamilton Baal, was elected to the U.S. House of Representatives (Dem., Cal.) at an early age, and the family treasure chest continued to swell. Swanson sired Harry Hamilton Baal, who followed his father's political footsteps and was elected to the U.S. Senate (Dem., Cal.). Harry was as astute as his father in his political dealings, and it wasn't long before he established the first of six Baal National Banks. Harry Hamilton, Jr., worked in the family banks until he was appointed to the U.S. Senate to fill a vacancy created when his father retired mid-term. Harry Jr. was appointed by the governor of California, at the time also a vice-president of the Baal National Bank of California who had put his bank holdings in a blind trust to avoid any possible conflicts of interest that might arise during his service as governor. Harry Jr. was subsequently elected to the Senate (Dem., Cal.) in his own right, without opposition, and a year later sired Harry Hamilton "J.J." Baal III. Aside from his father, J.J. was the sole surviving Baal, and his future was fixed by tradition. The year J.J. ran for governor, Harry Jr. was up for reelection, and they ran on the common slogan: COVER THE BASES FROM WASHINGTON, D.C., TO SACRAMENTO (D.C.), VOTE BAAL AND BAAL.

As J.J. became more aggressive, his prey became more submissive. Light petting turned to heavy petting, then to thrashing. After a few moments of thrashing, the two ran hand in hand into the woods, located several acres to the rear of the Baal estate. What followed need not be related here. However, the Baal family maid, Missie Jefferson, a forty-year-old mulatto with the voice of a ten-year-old, witnessed the entire episode with wide-eyed interest.

3

Missie had come west with Daphne when she married the senator. Missie was more a companion to Daphne than a servant; they had grown up together in Mobile and been close for the past thirty years. Daphne refused to spend any time in Washington with the senator, preferring the solitude of the Baal estate. And with J.J. away at school most of the year, she and Missie were usually the sole occupants of the Baal mansion. Daphne spent most of her time lounging in various rooms, always dressed as if she were awaiting a call to star in the remake of *Gone With the Wind*.

"Miss Daphne! Miss Daphne!" Missie shrieked, as she ran into the house. "Miss Daphne, where is you?"

Daphne lay on a divan, propped up with large satin pillows and nursing the headache that started twenty years earlier—on her wedding night. She was dressed in a full-length, bright green velvet dress with a fresh-cut, red rosebud pinned above her left breast and green satin slippers on her feet. She was a beautiful woman with long brunette hair that curled slightly, and the permanent frown did not detract from her beauty. "I'm in here, Missie, in the sitting room. Good Lord, what is the matter?"

Missie burst into the room. "Miss Daphne, oh, Miss Daphne," she wailed, wobbling on rubber legs.

"Lord, what is it, Missie?"

"Miss Daphne. Oh! Oh! Oh, Miss Daphne! J.J. and that boy Georgie Mandrocci is doin' terr'ble bad things."

"Don't tell me he's smoking cigarettes again."

"Oh, no, Miss Daphne, it worse than that!"

"Cigars?" said Daphne, raising her eyebrows. Missie just stared at her. "Not marijuana!" Daphne's voice rose to a high pitch as she sat up.

"No, Miss Daphne, it ain't tobacco or even marijuana that's smokin'." Missie's voice lowered to a mutter as she studied the

4

floor. "J.J. and that boy Mandrocci . . . , that boy and J.J., they been in the back woods scronchin'!"

"Schronchin'? *Schronchin'!*" Daphne yelled, slipping back to her southern drawl and satin pillows and reaching for her throbbing temples.

With some prodding from Daphne, Missie related all the sordid details, beginning with the lawn swing and ending with J.J. and Georgie romping and rolling in the woods, stark naked.

"Lord, Lord," Daphne muttered, "with that little Italian. That little *black* Italian! That Catholic!"

Missie walked over and sat on the foot of the divan, her hands folded in her lap. "Oh, Lord," moaned Daphne, "and I thought J.J. was so cute when he lost his first tooth and said he wanted to stay up all night so he could play with the *Tooth Fairy.* I even wrote it down in his baby book! Oh, oh, oh Lord." She took her hand from her head and looked at Missie. "We musn't tell the senator. We musn't let him know," she said pointedly, her voice under control.

"But he need to know," said Missie, shaking her head. "He gots to know!"

"NO! NO! NO! Missie. He'll want to have another son, and I can't do that *thing* in bed again. I just can't," she cried, her headache intensifying. "And what if we had a girl! It might never end. He'd want to do it again and again until he had a *real* son to carry on the tradition."

After some discussion, Missie agreed to keep their secret, and though she didn't have to, Daphne agreed to provide Missie with a modest but livable cash subsistence upon her retirement and until her dying day.

A few days later the spring recess ended, and J.J. and Georgie Mandrocci blissfully boarded a plane to fly east, returning to the exclusive boys' school that both attended. Daphne didn't discuss the incident with J.J. until he was preparing to graduate and told her that he intended to go into medicine—as a nurse, specializing in "male pediatrics." Daphne told him that she was well aware of his proclivity for the male gender and that if he knew what was good for him, he would follow in his father's footsteps until she was past her period of menopause. J.J. took the advice, and by the time her headaches ceased, he was running for governor and thoroughly enjoying the life of a politician. After his election night speech, a photograph flashed around the country: the three of them, their hands joined and held high in the air, with broad, toothy smiles across their faces—J.J. in victory, the senator in patrician glory, and Daphne in freedom from her cerebral bondage. The bases were covered from Washington, D.C., to Sacramento (D.C.), soon to become Sacramento, D.C. And J.J.'s only concern was how he would perpetuate the tradition.

At the precise moment that J.J. was romping and rolling with Georgie Mandrocci, his future adversary was being sworn in as the youngest sheriff in the history of Sacramento County. Chester Alfred "Buck" Mullins raised his right hand to take the oath of office three days after his thirty-fourth birthday. His boss and predecessor, Sheriff Henry Lukins, had died of a heart attack a week earlier while *touring* Mustang Ranch in Nevada. Reporters were rebuked by Mrs. Lukins when they questioned the propriety of the deceased sheriff's presence at Mustang Ranch, a bordello.

"I don't know what all the fuss is about," she said indignantly. "It's just a little old farm where they raise little old ponies, isn't it? He went there every now and then to horse breeders' conventions."

Chester was born in a little cotton-picking town in central Oklahoma. Shortly after turning eighteen, he migrated to Texas, staying just long enough to bend his Oklahoma accent toward that of a Texan, and somewhere between Dallas and Sacramento, he changed his nickname from Chet to Buck. Buck Mullins of Dallas, Texas, envisioned important doors swinging open for him when he introduced himself. However, he found that for him all the important doors swung out, and the only ones that swung in were at the rear of restaurants where he landed jobs washing dishes.

When Buck turned twenty-one, down and out, he signed on as a deputy with the Sacramento County Sheriff's Department. Upon meeting Sheriff Lukins, he went into his routine. "Proud to meet ya', Sher'ff," he said with his practiced accent, reaching out with his right hand. "Buck Mullins of Dallas, Texas."

"Dallas, Texas? You sound more like a damned Okie to me, Mullins," Lukins replied. "Matter of fact, I'd guess central Oklahoma, where I'm from."

"Why, yes . . . ye-yes, sir," Buck stammered. "Matter of fact, I was born and raised in Pottawatomie County. A little place called Tater, not too far from Maud. I only said I was from Dallas 'cuz that's the last place I lived. You probably never heard of Tater . . . right near Maud. You heard of Maud, ain't ya', sir?"

"Well, hell, Mullins," said Lukins, a smile growing on his face, "I got kin in Tater—my wife's cousin. Ain't never been there but sure know where it's at. My wife's cousin is Billy Haskins. Ever hear of 'im?"

"Oh, hell yes," Buck replied enthusiastically. "He's a good ol' boy. Runs the Exxon station out on the highway. Pumpin' gas, drinkin' beer, and tellin' good stories. Yeah, he's a damn good ol' boy."

"Small world, small world," the sheriff mumbled. Then, with a frown, "You ever pick cott'n, Mullins?"

"Hell yes, Sher'ff!" said Buck with a big grin. "Everybody in Tater picked cott'n. Picked cott'n till our asses were draggin'."

"Good, good. Ain't no som'bitch worth his salt that ain't picked cott'n. You're gonna do all right, boy. Yes, sir. You picked cott'n, you're gonna do ALL RIGHT!"

Buck did all right. He took night classes, studied diligently, passed his promotional exams, and "kissed a lotta asses." Buck was described by various people as a bullshitter, a born politician, a prevaricator, and, by most, a damned liar. But he was Sheriff Lukins' favorite *boy*. He'd picked cotton. Buck made captain at age thirty-two. Sheriff Lukins, eighty-one at the time, had no plans for retirement. He was determined to go out with his boots and badge on.

To speed the process along, Buck started sending the ancient lawman on frequent trips to Mustang, paying all expenses. At first it was every three or four months, but in the six months before Lukins died, Buck bankrolled seven trips. He was getting anxious.

The intent of this philanthropy was obvious to Lukins. On his last trip he told the three prostitutes in his room, "I know what he's doin', but what the hell. All you pretty ladies, all the Jack Daniels I can drink." He hoisted the bottle and slugged down a double shot. "Hell, I'm in TALL COTTON!" Five minutes later he was dead.

The funeral took place after three days of mourning and four days before the name of his replacement was announced. Buck told a friend, "If I don't get that job, it ain't no fault of mine. I passed more damn tests and kissed more damn asses than any man west of the Pecos." His love of affectionate rumps paid off when he finally achieved his dream. Buck Mullins became a genuine western sheriff.

8

Buck wasted no time in preparing for office. Within a week he had assaulted every western clothing store within fifty miles and filled his closet with the finest custom-made outfits that his credit could buy. For his size-13 feet, he bought Tony Lama and Justin boots made of everything from cowhide to South American snakeskins. Buck was a big man—six feet four and 264 pounds—but his boots, with built-in lifters and two-inch heels, boosted him to six feet seven and a half. He was indeed a towering, attractive figure. Wherever he went, everybody recognized Sheriff Buck Mullins.

Though he seldom wore it, Buck did not neglect his uniform. He had four large gold stars on each shoulder and more campaign ribbons on his chest than Audie Murphy and Haile Selassie combined. How he earned the ribbons, no one knew or ever asked. For his official photograph, he considered wearing a steel helmet, but after serious opposition from his wife, he agreed that it would not be quite proper.

Buck had a tall, thin, raven-haired wife and sired one child, Chester Alfred Mullins, Jr. For many years he was known as Little Buck, but this was later changed to Buster. Buster grew rapidly and by the time he was nine, Buck had him lifting weights. When Buck became sheriff, Buster was twelve and looked like a model for a body-building advertisement.

Buster was at his father's side for the swearing-in ceremony. Immediately afterward, Buck told him, "Son, you just keep punchin' that iron and someday you'll be the second youngest man to become Sher'ff of this county."

Nine years later Buster became a deputy. Fifteen years after that, he was the highest-ranking captain in the department, anxiously awaiting Buck's next move. And he never picked cotton.

9

CHAPTER 2

SIXTEEN YEARS BEFORE he burned Atlanta to the ground, William Tecumseh Sherman, an army lieutenant and a surveyor, was hired by the original city fathers to lay out the streets of the new city of Sacramento. The city boomed during the Gold Rush of 1849 and then settled down for almost a century. During the Second World War, it prospered again with the influx of servicemen and prostitutes, and many of the brothel owners later became prosperous businessmen who contributed to the economic growth of the community. For many years the city alternately grew and floundered, but toward *the end*, while the surrounding suburbs enjoyed great prosperity, Sacramento went into its final period of stagnation. The city fathers attempted every rescue effort, even offering the suburban voters the *opportunity* to annex or consolidate, but the mice weren't attracted by the rancid cheese. The final *aggrandizement* came with more government and more politicians who contributed little but their exalted presence. By the time J.J. took office as governor, every-

11

one in the city worked for the government or was on welfare or enjoyed both. Sacramento was a government town!

Although J.J. was only thirty-nine years old when he delivered his inaugural address, the thick silver-gray hair at his temples instilled in the voters a confidence that their young leader had the maturity to carry out the awesome responsibilities of his office. Immediately after completing his speech, he called a press conference and performed his first official act as governor by signing an executive order that required the posting of signs throughout the capitol grounds, advising: DOGS AND REPUBLICANS KEEP OFF THE GRASS. After much hearty laughter and a round of applause from the reporters present, all joined in a champagne toast to J.J.'s future success. After the inaugural festivities, J.J. flew to India to spend six weeks in meditation and cohabitation with a guru.

Upon returning to California, encouraged by his campaign slogan and with help from the city fathers and the state legislature, J.J. designated the city a state district and renamed it Sacramento, D.C. (District of California). This pleased everyone, for now the city government and services would be fully funded by the state treasury, and all city government officials received an immediate increase in pay. The only person upset by the move was Sheriff Buck Mullins, whose salary was now lower than that of the chief of police. By state law, he could not receive a raise during his present term of office. When word of Buck's irate jealousy reached J.J., he gave the chief another raise, setting off a feud that would come to a head three years later.

"That li'l som'bitch. That li'l turd kicker," fumed Buck. "I'm the sher'ff of one of the biggest sher'ff's departments in the state, the country, the whole damn world, an' he's tryin' to embarrass me, an' he ain't a gonna get away with it!"

J.J. rejected all the trappings of his office. The fleet of executive Cadillacs was melted down, sculpted into something resembling a giant cow patty, and exhibited in the capitol rotunda as a token of the frugality of his administration. The governor's mansion was rented out for one dollar a year to the United Farm Workers of America, to be used as an office for its president, Luigi "The Grape" Bambino, who, with some Mafia assistance, had taken over the union several years earlier. Opting for less luxuriant surroundings, J.J. rented a small apartment near the capitol and drove to work in either an old Datsun 210 or a motor scooter, depending on the occasion and the weather. He had the opulent furniture removed from his office and replaced with a metal desk and chairs painted battleship gray, and a few oversized pillows covered with burlap were scattered about the floor. The only "decorations" to break up the spartan surroundings were signed photographs of Jane Fonda, Daniel Ortega, and Kim Philby.

J.J. maintained a low-key approach to government affairs: "Have patience and we shall endure" was one of his favorite and often quoted sayings. His reputation as a handsome bachelor, rich but frugal, youngest governor of the largest state in the union, along with his unorthodox and sometimes mysterious ways, made him well known throughout the United States within a short period of time. In his third year as governor he began to travel extensively around the country, particularly to New Hampshire, and it soon became obvious that the only formality standing between him and a run for the presidency was his reelection as chief executive of the state of California. But by summer that formality began to take on the characteristics of a contest.

Sheriff Buck Mullins, tiring of his role as kingpin of Sacramento County, had aspirations of his own that required the removal of J.J. from office. Besides that, he hated J.J. Now, Buck was an old country boy and a damned liar. The people who *knew* him laughed at him, but those who knew *of* him were impressed. A lot of people knew of him, enough to make him a realistic threat to J.J. Buck was fifty-eight years old and had fifty-eight years of practice as a politician—five as a novice, sixteen as an amateur, thirteen as a semipro, and twenty-four as a professional.

"That little faggot might have the polish," he told a friend, "but when it comes to nut-cuttin' time, I can stand in there with the best of 'em."

Buck could be brutal if he had the material, and he had proven his ability in past campaigns. J.J. was aware of this and so was his chief of staff, Red Ainess, and both were worried. They didn't know what Buck knew or if he knew anything at all, but they were worried.

CHAPTER 3

DURING THE YEARS when Sacramento was a thriving community, its populace enjoyed the luxury of two daily newspapers. The majority subscribed to the paper which extolled the liberal point of view, while the remainder embosomed the conservative publication. But when Sacramento finally flopped over and became a full-fledged government town, the center of all political activity in the state, there was no longer a need for more than one point of view. There was only one point and one view, so the two papers joyfully merged under the masthead of the dominant *Sacramento Bunion.*

The Bunion Building, located a few blocks from the capitol, towered over the city. Housed within this Brobdingnagian container, which had the appearance of a coffin standing on end, were not only the offices of the daily *Bunion* but also an FM radio station (KROK-FM), an AM radio station (KROK-AM), a television station (KROK-TV), and six weekly newsshoppers that were distributed throughout the metropolitan area. The Bunion Company (not a dreaded corporate octopod), a family-run enterprise

15

founded by an early Sacramento pioneer, Jonathan A. McReynolds, was presently under the stewardship of Jonathan A. McReynolds III. To his friends, Jonathan III was simply J.A. J.A. and J.J. were friends, enjoying a common left-wing political philosophy. Between election years, however, J.J. was just more shark food. When it came to selling newspapers, J.A. didn't play favorites.

J.A. III was proud of the family company, which provided its employees with low pay but cradle-to-grave benefits—birth plans, death plans, and everything in between, all administered and doled out by the Bunion Company. On the various floors in the giant building were a medical clinic, grocery store, clothing store, department store, amusement center, barbershop, and beauty salon. It was often said and never disputed that a person could be born there, live there, and die there. It is not known if anyone was ever buried there.

The *Bunion* newsroom was located on the top (eighteenth) floor of the Bunion Building. The outside walls were all floor-to-ceiling tinted window glass, which at one time gave the occupants a beautiful view of the city and its thousands of trees. But with the arrival of Axel Rodd as city editor, all that changed. One of his first decisions was to have the newsroom windows painted black so that his reporters would more dutifully attend to their work. The layout and decor left the distinct impression that the entire massive room was designed, decorated, and furnished by someone trained and employed by some federal bureaucracy. Clusters of old scratched metal desks were scattered about the floor in groups of three or four. Some were face to face and some end to end, and others were face to end and end to face. Some were painted gray, the rest olive green (U.S. Army and Navy surplus). The remaining Bunion Building offices were a modern decorator's dream, with color-coordinated paint, furnishings, desks,

16

and typewriters, as was the newsroom until the advent of Axel. When he reported for work on his first Monday with the *Bunion*, Axel ordered the newsroom *remodeled*. It took four days to carefully remove all of the modern desks, chairs, and typewriters and pull up the matching wall-to-wall carpeting. On Friday the replacements were scattered and the banged-up, ten-year-old manual typewriters distributed. The windows were painted black by 5 P.M.

The following Monday, Axel announced to the gathered staff of reporters, "The days of the country club are over; it's time to go to work!" This was punctuated by a sonorous and resounding expulsion of intestinal gas that caused his baggy pants to flutter. It had to be a record setter, and his audience broke into a cheer and an extended round of applause. Without changing the stolid expression on his face, Axel turned and, as he started toward his office, delivered an encore of equal magnitude.

The former city editor had retired shortly before the merger, and two months later, after a nationwide search, J.A. McReynolds III proudly announced to his board of directors that he had found a highly qualified replacement. "Any man who would peddle pictures of his nude sister," J.A. beamed, "is a man with the guts it takes to run a first-class newspaper. A man that won't back away from anything. That man is Axel Rodd, the new captain of our mighty ship, who will continue to guide us through the purest waters in the highest journalistic tradition."

Axel was thirty-six when he became city editor but looked fifty-six, was shaped like an inverted pear, and therefore had to wear both a belt and suspenders. If he had a neck, you'd have to take his word for it. His head appeared to sit directly on the midline between his shoulders. Born in Palestine, Illinois, Axel was christened Alexander David Rodenberg. His parents, Grace and Harold, were highly respected members of the community, where Harold owned and operated a high-class and profitable jewelry store. Axel's one sister, Debra, a dark-haired lithesome beauty, was two years younger.

After studying agriculture and animal husbandry at the University of Illinois, Champaign-Urbana, Axel moved to Chicago, changed his name, and began to publish pornography, thus laying the groundwork for a successful future in journalism. His college training was not wasted—all his magazines featured farms, farmers, animals, and naked women. For two years his business ran smoothly. Then Axel made a mistake. He convinced Debra that the road to Hollywood started in Chicago, posing for one of his magazines. She was featured in the centerfold of *Young Mac-Donald's Farm* wearing only a cowgirl hat and sitting sidesaddle on a bareback, white-faced steer. After a copy made the rounds in Palestine, Axel's father put out a contract to have him killed, which he withdrew only after Axel agreed to leave the state for good and to never, even upon his death, use his family name for any purpose. Axel moved to Los Angeles and reviewed X-rated films for a tabloid, and pretty soon Debra started showing up in his reviews. Her dream had come true.

Axel's office was located in the corner of the newsroom, with a large window in one wall that looked out over the entire floor and offered an unobstructed view of all the reporters at their desks. A rolled-up shade could be pulled down for privacy, but Axel enjoyed the atmosphere of intimidation that he knew his observable presence provided. The one office adjacent to Axel's was occupied by his immediate boss, the managing editor. This office also had a window, but the shade was always drawn. No one ever saw the occupant of this office; in fact no one even knew his name. Only through notes, handwritten with red pencil, was his presence felt. Always critical, the notes to Axel and to various reporters were piled high on the secretary's desk each morning. Referred to as the *Evil Spirit,* this mysterious man created such fear that no one ever dared to try to snare him and prove that he was anything more than a red pencil.

Stationed in front of the two offices was the secretary, Judee Rose, who served both Axel and the managing editor. Like everyone else, Judee never saw or heard the Evil Spirit; to her he was a pile of red-penciled notes that she routinely delivered each morning.

A beautiful woman in her early thirties, Judee had shoulder-length auburn hair, bright green eyes, and a stunning 36(C)-26-36 figure in a tight sweater or blouse—from the left side. Unfortunately, she was flat-chested on the right, having lost her right breast in a traffic accident. Judee refused to wear a padded bra, which caused her to be unemployed for two years after the loss. She was on the verge of suicide when Axel hired her.

The reporters called her Uniboob, but Axel was impressed. "If a woman could have balls, she'd have 'em," he said. "Who the hell is to judge that one tit ain't as good as two, anyway! Leastways, she's honest. Some of these damned broads runnin' around here got nothin' but two piles of foam rubber and cotton under their blouse. What Judee shows is what Judee got. I like that."

But Judee was not a man and did not have "balls." She was very much a woman, one who was quite proud of her single, perfectly developed breast and who dressed in such a manner that it was always prominently displayed. Axel convinced her that she should pose nude in a full-color centerfold "for the betterment of unibreasted women across this country." She consented, but when the photographer could not get the desired effect, unibreasted

19

women lost their chance for "betterment," and Axel lost a fat commission check.

Axel spent most of his waking hours in his office, always arriving before sunup and always leaving last, long after the final edition was put to bed. He rarely saw his wife, Beatrice, and their eighteen-year-old, out-of-work, out-every-night son, Dorkas Rodd, slept late every day. If Axel saw him at all, it was on those weekends that he didn't go to the office. From the time Dorkas was sixteen, Axel referred to him as the Sloth, which Dorkas took as a compliment and adopted.

"But *Dorkas* is a girl's name," protested Beatrice when Axel chose the name. "It's Greek, the Romans used it, it's in the Bible. It's always been female."

"Beatrice," Axel said in a patronizing tone, "all little boys are dorks. It's in the dictionary, so Dorkas he is. Shows ya how much those Greeks and Romans know. Plus you can't believe what you read in the Bible."

"Dictionary of American Slang, you heathen," Beatrice muttered, lodging her final protest.

Beatrice was cute, eighteen, and a virgin when Axel met and married her. A year later, after bearing the Sloth, her attractive little rump began to slowly grow and spread, and in a few years she was also pear shaped, though with her it was stem end up. By the time she turned forty, her legs were purple varicose stumps and she had adopted European-style furry armpits.

Axel and Beatrice routinely threatened to throw each other out, but her need of his money and his desire to stay out of jail kept them together. After developing the Evil Spirit sham, Axel needed someone he could trust to write the notes—Beatrice. In a short period of time she got so good at it that she no longer needed his help. She took special pleasure in writing the ones

20

that cursed Axel; and she reminded him on a regular basis that if she were not his wife, nothing would stand between him and the jailhouse door.

Axel discovered the opportunity to more than double his income within days of taking the job as city editor. When he tried to locate the managing editor to introduce himself, he found that no one knew where or even who he was. J.A. remembered meeting him once, but that was all. Axel finally ascertained that the man had died at home six months earlier, but no one informed the *Bunion* and no one at the *Bunion* ever missed him. So Axel prepared the proper paperwork, using a fictitious name, and he "hired" a new managing editor. He ordered the payroll office to deposit all checks into a checking account that Axel had opened under the fictitious name. Each payday, Axel wrote a check to Beatrice that cleaned out the account. Should the scheme ever be discovered, Axel hoped that she would be the one sent to the slammer.

Axel didn't smoke or drink. Aside from thievery, his only vice was prune juice. He drank it like water and before going to sleep each night, he guzzled a full quart, which helped drive him out of bed every morning at 3 A.M.

CHAPTER 4

T O DESCRIBE RED AINESS, J.J.'s chief of staff, as haggard and worried-looking the day he *crawled* into Axel's office would be putting it mildly. For once, Axel pulled down his window shade, fueling speculation about the seriousness of the visit. An hour later, Red Ainess left and Axel raised the shade. From his beet-red face, it was obvious that he was mad enough to eat raw, bloody meat, and within moments, everyone knew who was going to provide the feast.

"JUDEE! Get that son of a bitch Stoney Gilson! Find the bastard! Tell him to get his rotten ass in here NOW!"

Stoneham "Stoney" Gilson was an intelligent, educated, honest, and smart-dressing journeyman reporter—an anomaly at the *Bunion*. With his round plastic-framed glasses, modest sport-coats and ties, white shirts, and short-cropped hair, Stoney looked like an Ivy League professor, and the mere mention of his name caused Axel to erupt in burning hives. Although the two were often at odds, Stoney didn't really dislike anybody, and that was something Axel simply couldn't fathom.

"The son of a bitch has got to hate somebody—his mother, somebody," Axel had been heard to rage on more than one occasion.

Judee, her breast bouncing precipitously, ran from one office to another until she found Stoney in the barbershop, getting his weekly trim.

"Stoney," she yelled, stopping to catch her breath. "Stoney, Axel wants you in his office—now!"

"Take it easy, Judee," Stoney calmly replied. "What does the *good* man want this time?"

"I don't know. He just yelled for you to get your A-S-S into his office. Red Ainess was in there. He even pulled his shade, and when Mr. Ainess left, Axel went crazy, cussing and yelling."

"Sounds normal to me," Stoney said. "Tell him I'll be there in about thirty minutes, after I get my shoes shined."

"Oh, Stoney, that will really make him mad."

In exactly forty-five minutes Stoney strolled into Axel's office, looking calm and relaxed from head to toe. Axel was sitting and seething behind his desk, with a malicious grin on his face and clenched fists resting on his prune-juice-stained blotter. "You said thirty minutes," hissed Axel through gritted teeth. "It's been forty-five, you agitating bastard."

"Come, come, Axel. You know I'm not a clock watcher, and you know I detest profanity. So please watch your mouth."

"Fuck you and your goddamned clock, Gilson."

Stoney, smiling, looked at the ceiling and then at Axel, raising his foot in the air for him to see. "Nice shine, huh?"

"Keep it up, Gilson. Keep it up and I'll shove that damn foot up your pompous ass."

"Okay, Axel, I give up. Now that you have again impressed me with your invective oral excrement, what do you want?" Actually

Stoney knew what Axel wanted. He was just surprised that it hadn't come sooner, when he first started doing background research on the governor.

"Who put you up to it?" said Axel, glaring. "That goddamned Okie sheriff?"

"Up to what? I don't know what you're talking about, Axel. And I haven't seen Buck for over a month."

"Okay, okay, wise guy. I want you off the governor's ass and I want you off his ass right now. You understand that, Mr. Wise Guy?" Axel yelled.

Stoney leaned forward and started to yell back, then leaned back and said with a smile, "I'm not on his 'ass,' as you put it, but from what I hear, he's not above that sort of thing."

"Now I know you've been talking to that Okie bastard. He's been spreading that bullshit all over the state 'cause he wants to run for governor. Trying to paint J.J. like he's some kind of homo or something. If he don't knock it off, he'll have his ass in a sling for slander."

"I'm not trying to paint *anybody* as *anything,*" Stoney replied calmly. "There's a lot of interest in our young bachelor governor's private life, and I intend to explore it."

"His private life is nobody's business, Gilson!"

"Axel, not too long ago you yourself stated that 'no politician has a private life.' "

"But he ain't no ordinary politician," Axel bellowed. "He's a statesman, and you don't drag a statesman through the mud of false accusations. He made us what we are today. Why California is almost like a country in itself. Making our capitol Sacramento, D.C.—that took genius. The man's a genius, presidential material. And someday that's what he'll be—president of the United States of America!"

"If Congress and the other states had their way, we *would* be a separate country," Stoney retorted. "They would have cut us loose long ago if the Constitution allowed it. And I don't intend to make any false accusations. Just truthfully present the facts. And that is a defense to libel."

"Don't hand me that lawyer shit. I decide what *truth* will be printed in this paper, and as of right now I'm ordering you off that story."

"Your order's good for three days, Axel. After that I'm on thirty days' leave of absence," Stoney grinned.

"Fine, fine," giggled Axel. "I'll cancel that bullshit, too."

"You can't do that," Stoney said. He reached into his inside coat pocket, took out a letter, and handed it to Axel. The letter, signed by J.A. McReynolds III, granted Stoney a thirty-day leave of absence, with the option to extend an additional thirty days. "It's in our guild contract, Axel. After ten years of service, we have an absolute right to sixty days' leave of absence every five years."

"Okay, okay," Axel said, but he was not quite ready to give up. "But what the fuck makes you such a persistent bastard when there's nothing there?"

"I'm just following your philosophy, Axel. Remember your little shark story? Or have you forgotten?"

When he first took over as city editor, Axel told his reporters to think of themselves as great white sharks. "If you smell blood, any amount, even a small drop, go for the kill—rip, tear, shred. But don't devour your prey. Let the ripped flesh lay and rot and stink for everyone to smell."

Axel, feeling trapped, grimaced. "Okay, okay, wise guy. First of all, that applies to Republicans—the flag-waving, mother-and-apple-pie, God-and-country gestapo bastards. But you'd better be right. You'd better have proof, or you'll get your fucking neck chopped off. You conservative, midwestern, moralizing little prick. Why I bet you're one of those meatheads who thinks Suzuki Honda is a Communist."

Suzuki Honda, a wealthy singer and recording star, founded the National Education Fund and Training Facility for the Development of a Young Democratic Peoples Republic of Amerika (N.E.F.T.F.D.Y.D.P.R. of A.).

"Oh, I've heard some stories. Plus the facts do speak for themselves," Stoney said, bored. "She's too dumb to take seriously, but to quote another old saying, 'If it walks like a duck, talks like a duck, and looks like a duck, it must be a duck.' And speaking of *ducks*, you know that your star female reporter and Wanda Flagella are sharing a house in the foothills, don't you?"

"What's wrong with two women sharing a house? I suppose the next thing you'll tell me is that Penny Penny and the chief justice of the California Supreme Court are a couple of lesbians."

Stoney smiled. "I don't know about the good Chief Justice Flagella, but I do know that your friend Penny Penny keeps a dildo in her purse, and . . ."

"All right, Gilson, I've heard enough of your horseshit for one day. The only connection is that they're all good friends. Penny and Wanda and the governor were classmates at Berkeley. And I don't care if that horny broad has six dildos in her purse."

"You didn't let me finish, Axel. I *saw* the dildo. Judee told me about it. One day when she and Penny were in the restroom together, she spotted it when Penny put her comb away. So when I got a chance, I peeked in her purse and there it was. A cute little thing." Stoney held up his index fingers about six inches apart. "And that's not all. It was hand-painted—excellently done—with little white daisies on the head and a bright royal blue 'WANDA' on the shaft."

"You gotta be lyin', Gilson. The broad couldn't be that dumb, but we'll soon find out. Judee!" he screamed. "Tell Penny to get her tail in here and bring her purse with her."

Moments later, Penny entered with a questioning look on her face and her purse in her left hand. Tall, thin, and pretty, Penny looked ten years younger than her thirty-eight. Unfortunately, her manner of dress always gave the impression that she just fell off the back end of a prairie schooner. When she entered the office, Axel began sniffing the air, turning his head from side to side. A strong odor flowed through his nostrils and ticked away at his memory bank of smells. "What the hell? What kind of perfume is *that?*"

Penny glared at Axel, glanced at Stoney, and then returned to Axel. "It's a gift . . . from Wanda . . . she loves it."

"What the hell *is* it?" Axel demanded, his nose quivering like a rabbit, sniffing loudly.

"Brut," said Penny.

Stoney threw his right hand to his mouth to smother a laugh and turned his head away from Axel and Penny.

"Brut? Brut!" Axel yelled. "Oh, goddamn! Why me, Lord, why me? Give me your purse and sit down," he demanded.

Penny, still glaring at Axel, complied without question. Axel grabbed the purse and dumped the contents on his desk. Penny, realizing what Axel was about to do, yelled for him to stop and then ran from the office. The last item to fall out was an excellently hand-painted dildo, with little white daisies on the head and "WANDA" on the shaft. Axel stared at the dildo in disbelief.

28

Looking up at Stoney, he said, "She'll be back. Give the dipshit a couple minutes to cry."

Axel and Stoney had sat in silence for a few minutes when Penny reappeared, red eyed but trying to look casual and proper.

"You rat," she said, staring at Axel. "Axel, you're a no-class rat."

"I might be a rat, but you've got to be the dumbest broad I ever laid eyes on. I studied animals in college and never found one as dumb as you. Now put all that shit back in your purse, and when you get home tonight, burn that goddamn thing." Looking at Stoney, he continued, "And don't tell this guy a damn thing. And forget that dildo ever existed."

"Don't look so damn smug, Gilson!" he bellowed. "You don't have nothin'. You're back to ground zero, and when you're through screwing around, you'll still be at ground zero."

Axel leaned back in his chair, thinking for a moment. "Judee," he yelled. "Judee, get Gassaway on the phone."

Axel leaned forward and pointed a finger at Stoney. "I know that goddamned Okie sheriff is mixed up in this thing someplace. You and him got something going, and I'm going to get a piece of his ass before it's all over."

"I'm not in on anything with Buck," Stoney mumbled.

"You can't lie worth a shit, Stoney," said Axel, his voice now calm in anticipation of his plan. "Penny, set up a personal interview with that tub of shit sheriff. I'll fill you in on what to ask him after asshole here is gone.

"As for you, Gilson, I don't know how you could hold an opinion of someone you know so little about. The governor is holding a news conference before you go on leave. Cover it. After you see what a genius this man is, I'm sure you'll agree with me and forget all this other bullshit. Now get your ass out of here and tell your fat sheriff friend hello for me." Axel grinned maliciously.

"So long, Axel," Stoney said. He was smiling as he walked out the door.

When Stoney was out of hearing distance, Axel averred, "One of these days that little prick's going to step in some shit that he won't be able to get out of. Now, for you, Penny," he said with a sympathetic smile.

"Yes, Axel." She had calmed considerably.

"About a year ago that hog jaw sheriff made some statement about renaming San Francisco Sodom-by-the-Sea and how someday it would fall into the ocean. Nobody did anything with it, but now I'm going to shove it down his throat. When you talk to him, bait him real good. Suck some good quotes out of him. Get him going on that Sodom-by-the-Sea shit. We'll make him look like the dumb loon he is. When we get through, he'll be lucky to get elected dogcatcher. And for insurance I'm going to hang *Crotch* around his neck like a ten-ton rock. Tell Harmony that I want her to get on that right away. Never mind. Tell her to see me, and I'll tell her how to handle Crotch."

"But Crotch is a crime story," Penny protested. "Gassaway is covering that."

"Not anymore," snorted Axel. "That little shit is more cop than he's reporter. That dumb Okie has been trying to catch Crotch for two years, and Gassaway makes him look like some kind of supersleuth. Well, that's all over. We're going to show how inept that scumbag really is."

At that moment the intercom buzzed. Judee said that Harrison Gassaway was on the phone.

Harrison Gassaway had worked for the *Bunion* for twenty-eight of his fifty-two years. For the last twenty-six of those twenty-eight years, he was assigned to the police beat, covering all crime news from the police and sheriff's departments. Harrison, who spent all his time at the offices of the police and sheriff, had not set foot in the Bunion Building for nearly a quarter of a century. He phoned in his stories and only knew Axel through their conversations on the phone. Harrison never met or talked to a man he didn't like except for Axel Rodd. He liked everyone and everything. In three years he could retire, and he counted every day.

"Gassaway," Axel yelled into the phone, "this is Rodd."

"Yes, Axel, I *do* recognize your voice."

"Gassaway, I'm taking you off the Crotch story," Axel said very matter of factly. "From now on, Harmony will cover Crotch."

"You can't do that to me," Gassaway cried. "Harmony's a damn rookie. You're kicking me in the nuts, Axel."

"I know I'm kicking you in the nuts, Gassaway. You need to be nut-kicked. I want some good copy on Crotch, not that watered-down shit you've been sending in. At least a rookie will do what I tell her to do."

"You're making me look like a fool, Axel. It's bad enough that you're taking the story away, but to give it to a rookie is a gross insult," Gassaway moaned, angry tears welling up in his eyes.

"Look here, Gassaway. I'm sick and tired of this Crotch character running around and terrorizing the community. I want him caught. He's hit my house twice. How do you think my wife feels knowing that some wild man is out there running around loose with two crotches that he cut out of her pantyhose? The only way he's going to be caught is to put heat on that ignorant pig sheriff.

And to do that I need *good* copy, and you don't seem to know what that is."

"I won't shade a story for anybody, Axel," Gassaway cried. "We have our credibility to worry about."

"Credibility, horseshit! The idiots out there don't have memories. They get mad today and forget it tomorrow."

"You're putting me down. Putting me down real bad, Axel," whimpered Gassaway, defeated. "I'm going to look like an old fool."

"I'm through arguing with you, Gassaway!" Axel screamed, spraying saliva all over the mouthpiece. "You're a fool. A fucking worthless old fool. That's why you're a no-class, fucking, police beat reporter. Now just shut up and go back to pounding leather and sending in your worthless little crime stories." He slammed the phone into its cradle, cracking the plastic.

Gassaway stumbled out of his little cubbyhole in the basement of the police station, across the hall from the armory, mumbling to himself. "Three more years," he groaned. "Three more long years." He looked in the armory and stared at all the shotguns and pistols in their racks. Finding no one there to talk to, he started to leave, thinking about retirement years and his quadriplegic wife. Halfway out the door he turned, walked back in, lifted a .357 magnum from the rack, loaded it, stuck it in his mouth, and pulled the trigger.

A few minutes later, the officer in charge of the armory returned to find Gassaway, still standing, straight and stiff as a board, with the gun still in his mouth. "What in the hell are you doing, Gassaway," the officer said. "You dipshit, those guns are all broken. And the next time you wanna try and kill yourself, do it somewhere else. I don't want your blood and brains all over my fucking armory."

CHAPTER 5

THE FIRST KNOWN CROTCH attack occurred at 2 A.M. in a wealthy suburb of Sacramento, D.C. Dr. Wilson W. Wilson and his wife had just retired for the night when they heard their garbage cans rattle.

Mrs. Wilson immediately sat up in bed and shook her half-asleep husband. "Did you hear that, Willy?"

"Oh, go to sleep, Winnie," he answered in a disgusted tone of voice. "It's just those damn dogs again. Damn animals. Damn people who let them run loose. I'll clean up the mess in the morning."

Dr. Wilson was a nationally known psychiatrist who made millions from his books on psychotherapy and predicting human behavior. Though he had never treated a single patient, he read and reread every volume ever published on mental disorders and paraphrased them in his publications.

A few minutes later, Winnie raised up again. "I hear someone in the kitchen," she whispered.

"Oh, bullshit, Winnie," Willy mumbled sleepily. "Lie down and go to sleep. Damn!"

"How can I sleep with someone in our kitchen? Darn you, Willy, go look. Call the police. Do something."

"Okay, okay." Willy slipped out of bed and walked to the kitchen. He opened the door, ran his hand over the wall, found the switch, and turned on the overhead light. He blinked a couple of times, getting used to the light, and then saw what was to become the terror of Sacramento, D.C., leaning against the refrigerator door and calmly sipping a Dr. Pepper. The intruder was wearing a bright green windbreaker, blue jeans, sneakers, black leather gloves, and a ski mask.

"What in the hell are you doing here?" Willy exclaimed.

"Just havin' me a Dr. Pepper," answered the masked man.

Willy studied him for a moment. "Well, when you're finished, throw your empty in the trash and be sure to lock the door on your way out." With that, Willy returned to the bedroom.

The doctor's frightened wife was cowering on the bed. "Well, what's going on?" she asked.

"The young man is having a can of Dr. Pepper. Now go to sleep, Winnie, please."

"Go to sleep! There's someone in our kitchen. He could be a maniac. A murderer. A rapist. Aren't you going to do something?"

"Stop it, Winnie. I'm the expert on human behavior around here," he said matter of factly. "Now listen to me and then go to sleep. I told him to be sure and clean up his mess and to lock the door on his way out. Now, if you're still awake when he leaves, please check the door to see that it's locked. Good night." With that, Willy went to sleep.

Thirty minutes later, Winnie heard the door open and close quietly. She slipped out of bed, tiptoed into the kitchen, and checked the door. It was locked. In the trash container under the sink were six empty Dr. Pepper cans. Winnie smiled and returned to bed with a renewed confidence in her Willy.

But the next morning they discovered the main object of the intruder's attack in their washroom, just off the kitchen. Laid out on the floor were two pairs of Winnie's pantyhose with the crotches neatly cut out and missing.

"He is a nut after all," Winnie cried. "He didn't just want a drink of Dr. Pepper. He's crazy. He deceived you, Willy." Her confidence in Willy was slipping again.

"Yes, yes. He's a crafty one all right," Willy proclaimed. "But what discipline. Did exactly as he was told. What capacity," Willy marveled. "Six cans in thirty minutes and never used the bathroom once. Must be very smart—very crafty!"

Crotch continued his attacks on a weekly basis so that by the end of his first year's activity, he had captured 104 pantyhose crotches and consumed approximately 312 cans of Dr. Pepper.

Only once did he commit an act of overt violence. Upon confronting one young lady, he found that she wore neither panties nor pantyhose and her refrigerator contained only Royal Crown Cola. Infuriated and perhaps disgusted, he tied her up and forced her to watch while he pulled the wing feathers out of her pet canary. The canary survived, but its feathers failed to grow back and it ended up a diplegic invalid. It later came to light that the lady was indeed a Dr. Pepper drinker, but the store where she shopped was out of her favorite beverage; further, just two days before the attack, her pimp had convinced her to get rid of all her panties and pantyhose.

When news of the canary episode spread, a panic developed among the thousands of pet bird owners in the community, and Sheriff Buck Mullins began to search desperately for a way to trap and capture Crotch. Finally, his son, Captain Buster Mullins, came up with a plan: remove all the Dr. Pepper from the area except for one house and then wait for him to show up.

"That boy of mine is a genius!" declared Buck. And the plan

was implemented. With the help of the local merchants, the entire supply of Dr. Pepper in the Sacramento, D.C., metropolitan area was depleted. When the last six-pack was sold, the following article appeared on the front page of the *Bunion:*

LAST CAN OF DR. PEPPER SOLD

To the dismay of Dr. Pepper lovers everywhere, the last can of Dr. Pepper in the D.C. area has been sold. It was purchased at exactly 5:30 P.M. yesterday. The lucky buyer, Miss Dawna Cape, lives alone with her pet canary, Phred, at 250 Bonita Street. Miss Cape, who works at home, is a pantyhose tester for the Stretchmore Pantyhose Company.

With the bait planted, Buster and his SWAT team spent seven anxious days and nights in the closets at 250 Bonita Street, armed with machine guns, but to no avail. During that week, Crotch struck three times, but not at 250 Bonita.

Crotch, evidently in response to the crisis, turned philanthropist. At each of the three houses, he took two crotches but left a six-pack of Dr. Pepper and the following note:

JUS A LITUL SOMTHING To Sho Mi APREESh-EASHUN i HAVE A Big SUPPLi

The following day, the merchants restocked their cold boxes with Dr. Pepper, and Crotch returned to his normal routine.

Six months later, Buck and his large staff of detectives assigned to the Crotch Detail were still floundering, with no physical evidence, no leads, and only a flimsy physical description. In desperation, Buck commissioned Dr. Wilson W. Wilson and a staff of other psychiatric experts to develop a psychiatric profile on Crotch. After thirty days of intensive study, Dr. Wilson released his report.

> After a thorough analysis of all available data, we have reached the following conclusions concerning the man known as Crotch: He is a paranoid schizophrenic but extremely intelligent. He is a highly motivated and aggressive personality type. He has a very domineering mother and docile father. His father is a low-key gentleman who has had little influence in Crotch's life. He probably has older brothers and sisters who attempt to dominate him. He is probably in his early twenties and physically agile. His obvious target analysis and tactical movements lead us to believe that he is either a highly trained military tactician or a genius with this natural ability. His approximate age leads us to believe that the latter is true. The notes he left were clever attempts to lead law enforcement officers to believe that he is of a lower mentality. The real danger of this man is that he may discontinue cutting pantyhose and start going for the real thing. If and when identified, he should be approached with extreme caution, as he could become overly aggressive and pose a danger to arresting officers.

After submitting his official report, Dr. Wilson immediately began preparing for his next book, paraphrasing all the police reports now in his possession and dreaming of the day that Crotch would be caught as a result of his expert analysis.

CHAPTER 6

S HERIFF BUCK MULLINS may have been born and raised in Tater, Oklahoma, but his *character* was developed in Dallas, Texas. He liked things big, Texas big, and the elephantine chamber that he called his office was no exception. Immediately upon becoming sheriff, he began knocking down and moving walls until he had a twenty- by forty-eight-foot room with plush, bright red, wall-to-wall carpeting and oak-paneled walls. His desk and chairs were positioned at one end, where business was conducted. At the other was an overstuffed, black leather sofa and two matching chairs, where more intimate conversations were held.

Buck's desk and chairs were custom-made so that he sat slightly higher than his visitors without it being obvious. His desk and personal chair were elevated an inch, while the legs of the other chairs were reduced a half inch, allowing him to look down upon his supplicants. Directly behind him, in floor stands, were the American flag, the Texas and California state flags, and his own custom-made "sheriff's" flag. The rest of the room and three of the walls were filled and covered with western memorabilia and

39

"antiques." There were tables fashioned from old wagon wheels, old rifles and sixshooters, a set of steer horns, and a polished horse collar with a mirror in its center. And in one corner, on a special saddle rack, sat a beat-up saddle reputed to have been used by the Texas Rangers.

Adorning the wall behind the sofa was a full-length oil painting of Buck—in full uniform, with pants bloused over military jump boots, a chest full of "campaign" ribbons, and a steel helmet boasting four large gold stars. Many a visitor, glancing at the painting, took the sheriff for a former army general, which was fine with Buck, whose military career consisted of a stint as a part-time cook in a Salvation Army soup kitchen in Dallas. Every office in the sheriff's department housed at least one picture of Buck—eleven- by fourteen-inch portraits—without the steel helmet. And all who entered his office exited with an autographed photo, whether they wanted it or not.

But Buck's real mania was plaques. Buck was a *plaque collector*. Eighty-two plaques blanketed one entire wall of his office. Of these, twenty-seven were given to him for various honors. The others Buck had made for himself for whatever honor he felt that he merited. Mirroring the plaques, on the opposite wall, was a large collection of personally autographed photographs from nationally known celebrities. Most started with "To my good friend Buck," and many bore strikingly similar handwriting.

To every admiring visitor, Buck announced that not one dime of taxpayers' money was invested in the furnishings, including the carpet. Nor was any of *Buck's* money invested in the furnishings, though he didn't mention that. Buck was an expert mooch, and his office allowed him to be an official mooch. "That sure would look nice in my office," he would say. If that failed, he would become a little more direct: "I'd sure like to have something like *that* for *my* office." Or, "Mind letting me *borrow* that?" Because Buck was very persuasive, almost every item in his office once belonged to a private party who didn't necessarily want to part with it. He even carpetbagged the carpet.

Buck did have one real passion, which was neither his marriage nor his possessions, however grand, nor even his position, which he zealously used and abused. No, Buck's only real passion was Bombay gin, which he bought by the case. There were no two- or three-martini lunches for Buck. If he didn't consume at least two shakers full, it was considered just a snack. When the call from Stoney came through, he had just returned from a full-course meal.

Buck was sitting behind his desk, staring at his plaques, when his private line rang. Buck never identified himself when answering his private phone until he knew who he was talking to. "Yeah?"

"Buck?"

"Who wants to know?"

"Buck, this is Stoney. Don't you recognize my voice? You're drunk again, aren't you?"

"I ain't drunk, goddamnit! There ain't enough Bombay gin in this entire town to get ol' Buck Mullins drunk."

"Well, I hope you're sober enough to understand when I tell you that Axel Rodd is going to try and nail your posterior to the wall."

"For the last time, I ain't drunk, goddamnit!" And he wasn't. Buck had capacity. "And that goddamn Axel Rodd ain't gonna do nothin' to my ass but kiss it!"

"He's pretty upset, Buck. He finally got wind of me backgrounding J.J., and he's convinced that you put me up to it. He's assigning Penny Penny to do a number on you, so be on the lookout."

"She already called," said Buck. "Got the message right here."

"Well, if you give her the interview, watch your step. Also, Gassaway called. Axel's taken him off of Crotch. Really gave him the business, then assigned a rookie, Harmony Nerd, to get on Crotch and make you look like a senile Wyatt Earp."

Buck leaned back in his chair and roared with laughter. "Well, it's going to take a helluva lot more than some rookie turd named Nerd to get ol' Buck! Listen, Stoney," he continued, "I'm gonna wait and see on that Crotch deal. If it looks like he's getting away with hangin' me, I'll use my big hammer and clean that Crotch mess up."

"Not . . . not Redneck and Watermelon!"

"That's it exactly," said Buck. "I don't like takin' that kind of chance, but if I have to, I will."

"Well, hold off and see what he does first," Stoney warned.

"Don't worry. I have to be desperate to let those two out of their cage," Buck agreed.

"Now I have to tell you something that you're not going to want to hear," Stoney said, cautiously. "I told Axel about Wanda."

"Wanda Flagella? About her and Penny?"

"No, Buck, I think he's known about that all along. What I told him about is Penny's Wanda—the dildo. He was giving me the business about J.J., and I wanted to jab him back a bit, so I told him about his pet reporter's plastic pet. He went nuts. Called her in, took her purse, dumped everything out on his desk, cussed her out, and then told her to burn it. So there goes your physical evidence. Should have grabbed that thing a long time ago," Stoney moaned.

"Shit, Stoney, she won't burn her little *Wanda*. She'll put it someplace, and we'll find it. I got ways. Besides, it ain't all that important. Of course, if I could get Flagella, it would sure help make that fuckin' J.J. look like a horse's ass for appointing her. Especially after the fiasco over that first dumb cunt he put in there."

J.J. had appointed Wanda chief justice of the state supreme court when his first appointment, Daisy Crow, committed suicide after being caught shoplifting a package of peppermint Certs in a Payless.

"Well, so far I haven't got a thing on J.J.," Stoney said. "But my leave starts in three days, and if there's anything there, I'll find it. A few years back I did a short piece on J.J.'s old man. They had a maid who was with them forever until they put her out to pasture. Now she's holed up in a little place called Lake Forest, near Mobile. I'm going there first thing."

"You oughta find somethin' on that little faggot som'bitch. That old gal will know. Wait and see," said Buck.

"Well, I'm still not convinced that you're right, Buck. He's got that girlfriend, Antoinette Mandrocci, that he's been sneaking around with. Matter of fact, she's flying out here in a couple of days, right after his big press conference. It's supposed to be a secret, but somebody leaked it, just like the last time."

"That's all bullshit, Stoney," Buck countered. "I know a fag when I see one, and that worthless little som'bitch is a flat-out fairy. The only thing that would give the little shit a hard-on is watching Superman do a striptease. This Mandrocci dame is a cover.

"By the way, Stoney," Buck continued, "she's from Alabama. Big-time model, beauty queen, former Miss Alabama. What the hell is his connection with Alabama?"

"His mother's from there," Stoney said. "Has a lot of friends and relatives down there."

"Well, she might be worth talkin' to."

"I doubt it, Buck. If she's sleeping with him, she won't talk to me."

"Shit, Stoney, if she's sleeping with that fag, she's a virgin, and virgins never lie."

"Okay, Buck," Stoney laughed. "I have to run. Remember Penny. Be careful with her. She hides a tape recorder in her purse. If she puts her purse on your desk, you can bet she's recording."

"Don't worry about me, Stoney. I've got ways and means to take care of this broad." He grinned.

"Go easy, Buck. A president was drummed out of office for some of the same things you've done."

"Shit, Stoney," Buck yawned, "the problem with that dumb som'bitch is that he thought he was above the law. Well, I *am* the law!"

"Oh, hell," Stoney mumbled to himself. "Goodbye, Buck. Be talking to you when I get back from Alabama."

"Take it easy, Stoney. In case I never told ya, I think you're a good ol' boy. Even though you ain't ever picked cott'n." Buck laughed.

"Thanks, Buck."

"Bye, Stoney." Buck grinned as he hung up the phone. He sat motionless for several minutes, then suddenly stood up, having decided to prepare for some very serious thinking. He would call Penny later.

Buck walked to the far end of his office and opened the door that led into his secretary's office.

"Brenda, honey, hold all my calls for a while," Buck said, mawkishly. "I've got some heavy thinking to do. Got some decisions to make. I'll let you know when I'm through."

"Sure thing, Sheriff Mullins," cooed Brenda. "I'll keep everything super quiet for you."

They smiled at each other like sweethearts as he returned to his office and locked the door. Buck was always extra nice to Brenda. She was not only very pretty, buxom, and a damn good secretary to boot, but her husband, Chuck Hudson, was the local distributor for Bombay gin. Brenda couldn't stand the sight of Buck, but he paid her well, and even at wholesale prices, Chuck made a few dollars selling Buck his gin.

Buck stood still for several minutes, breathing deeply, his eyes closed, preparing himself for what was his favorite part of almost every day. Then he marched to the far corner of the room, where the Texas Ranger saddle sat on its sturdy, custom-made stand, and mounted up. He sat for a moment, wide-eyed, both hands folded over the saddlehorn and both feet locked into the stirrups. He wiggled his buttocks, getting comfortable. Then he closed his eyes, and his body became rigid.

Soon he could feel the enormous surge of power in the muscles of the great white stallion between his legs as they charged through the Piazza Colonna in Rome, his brilliant white tunic fluttering in the breeze. Thousands of Romans cheered him from the balconies that lined the streets, but he ignored them. Instead, he charged on through the great Arch of Constantine and on to the Baths of Caracalla, where he brought the giant steed to a skidding halt and leaped from the saddle.

As he casually strolled into the mastodonic entry hall of the great Baths, he was met by three lovely maidens, dressed in diaphanous pastels. They led him to a private hall containing three beautiful pools that were surrounded by piles of soft cushions and baskets of fruit. After he had eaten and rested briefly, the three maidens undressed him, bathed him in one pool, rinsed him in the second, and had him soak and lounge in the third. After drying him off, they dressed him in a purple and gold tunic and escorted

45

him to a large, opulently furnished bedroom, where he was left alone to nap.

A short time later, his three beautiful concubines floated through the door, filling the room with the wonderful aroma of their bodies bathed in rich perfumes. They undressed him and teased him with their own naked bodies, and in the end he made love to all three. Then he fell asleep, exhausted.

He was awakened again, but this time by a young second lieutenant. "General Mullins, sir, it's time. It's 0400, sir."

Without hesitation, General Buck Mullins, Supreme Allied Commander, jumped from his bed fully dressed, grabbed his steel helmet with four stars, and went out to address his men. It was D-Day, June 6, 1944.

"Men," he declared, looking up and down the ranks, "you are about to embark upon a great crusade." And with those words, General Buck Mullins launched an attack that involved three million men, five thousand ships, four thousand landing craft, and eleven thousand aircraft. It was indeed an exhausting day, sending a spent General Mullins back to his quarters. But as he was dozing off, there was an explosion, and he was thrown from his bed.

When Buck opened his eyes, he was on the floor of his office. He stood up, leaned against the saddle, and stared at his plaques. It had taken him thirty minutes to win a horse race, fill himself with fruit, bathe with three maidens, take a nap, make love to three concubines, take another nap, and then launch the Battle of Normandy. Not a bad day at all. Buck couldn't remember the last time he'd made love to his wife, but between those plaques and that old saddle stood one smiling, satisfied, successful sheriff.

Whistling, almost skipping, Buck went to his office door, opened it, and purred, "Brenda, honey, get that Miss Penny Penny on the phone for me." He winked.

"Yes, sir, Sheriff Mullins," Brenda answered sugarsweetly. Then, with a slight touch of acid, she inquired, "Did your quiet time go well, or did that sonic boom ruin it all?"

"Sonic boom?" Buck paused a moment. "Oh, yeah, the sonic boom. No. No, it didn't bother me. Everything was just fine." He gave Brenda another wink as he walked back into his office. Within a few moments, Penny Penny was on the phone.

"Miss Penny, this is Sheriff Mullins returning your call. What can I do for you?" When talking to the press, Buck was both polite and mannered. He tried to drop his accent, his slang, and his profanities and use as many big words as possible. One of his favorites was *herculean*. Buck *was* educated. He'd worked hard for his Bachelor of Arts degree. Then, after he became sheriff, he picked up a master's by attending a few classes and having one of his brighter aides write his thesis.

"Why Sheriff, thank you for returning my call," purred Penny. "It's so nice to talk with you again. It's been such a long, long time."

"Yes, it certainly has, Miss Penny, and I must admit that I am the cause of the unfortunate decrement. I have made a herculean effort in the past to maintain favorable communications with professional journalists like yourself, and of course *others* in the media, but the expanding, mastodonic problems of running this office are almost prohibitive."

"Yes, I understand, Sheriff." Penny, trying desperately to suppress her laughter, nearly choked.

"Are you all right, my dear?" asked the suddenly sincere sheriff.

"Yes, yes, Sheriff. Fine. Just trying to hold back a sneeze." Penny regained her composure and continued. "Sheriff, I'm calling because I would like to interview you for a special feature in the *Bunion*."

"A feature on ME!" Buck exclaimed, trying to sound convincingly surprised. "Why on earth would anyone want to write about me? And who would read it?" Buck Mullins laughed the laugh of a born liar.

"Oh, Sheriff, don't be so modest," replied the born reporter and concubine to the chief justice. "Everybody is interested in the man who might be our next *governor*."

"Well, now, Miss Penny, that's all speculation and an enormous amount of canard," Buck protested, though not too vehemently. "I've heard those rumors for quite some time and have made a herculean effort to put them to bed."

"Just the same," countered Penny, "there is a *strong* possibility that you will run, and we want to be the first newspaper in the state to do a *good* story on you."

"I'll bet you would!" Buck exclaimed, remembering Stoney's admonition. "I mean," he recovered, "I'll bet you would do a good job."

"Thank you, Sheriff," Penny said, missing his first remark. "Can I take that to mean that you'll do the interview?"

"Yes, Miss Penny. I'll be glad to share some of my thoughts concerning the gargantuan problems facing our government today."

"Sheriff Mullins, I love you," squealed Penny, sensing the bait taken, the hook lodged firmly in the sheriff's cheek. "How about early next week?"

"No, I'm sorry, Miss Penny. That would be impossible. I have several herculean tasks before me that will take at least two weeks to dispose of," the sheriff lied in turn. "How about two weeks from today?"

"That will be splendid," giggled the reporter. "I'm sure that you and I will have a very enjoyable and informative visit. I'm certainly looking forward to seeing you again."

"Thank you, Miss Penny. You are a sweet lady, and I know

our visit will be most fruitful. Goodbye, dear. I'll see you in two weeks."

"Goodbye, Sheriff, and thank you again."

No sooner had his phone hit the cradle than Buck was yelling, ever so sweetly, to his secretary. "Brenda, honey, get that LaMarr Horsendork on the phone and tell him to get down here on the double."

"But, Sheriff, it is almost five o'clock. He may not be in."

"Call every sleazy bar, massage parlor, and strip joint in town if you have to, Brenda. I think the dummy carries a pager, so we oughta be able to get ahold of him."

After fifteen phone calls (no pager), Brenda located LaMarr at the police station, where he'd stopped by to catch up with old cronies. "He'll be here by five-thirty, Sheriff Mullins." Brenda batted her eyes, packed her purse, and left for home.

LaMarr Horsendork was a mess. He wasn't ignorant. In fact he was fairly intelligent. But he was a mess. A former Sacramento, D.C., policeman turned private investigator, LaMarr was also a flasher. He'd been in the department for about five years when he was arrested in San Francisco for flashing a female cable car operator late one night while crawling halfway to the stars. He was fired and hadn't been caught flashing since.

At promptly five-thirty, LaMarr entered Buck's office wearing a trench coat over a summer suit and black, wing-tip shoes with horseshoe taps covering the heels. LaMarr was a mess.

"LaMarr," snarled Buck, "what in the fuck are you doin' with a trench coat on in the middle of summer? You're not up to your old tricks again, are you?"

LaMarr shook his head. "No, Buck. I just felt a little chill comin' on, so I threw it on right before I came up here."

"I know you like to flash our elevator operator, you dipshit," said the sheriff. "And you know she won't turn you in. Is that what you did, LaMarr?"

"Aw, Buck, come on. . . ."

"LaMarr," Buck interrupted, "take that fuckin' coat off. Now!" LaMarr stared at him for a moment, then took the trench coat off and threw it on a chair. "Now zip up your goddamn pants and sit down over here," demanded Buck, pointing to one of the overstuffed chairs in the intimate conversation area. "You crazy goddamn German. Hitler's probably rolling over in his fucking grave."

"I'm not German, Buck, as I've told you more than once," LaMarr frowned. "My father came from Yugoslavia. Nikola Horsendorkich. He dropped the 'ich' when he got off the boat." LaMarr sat down.

"Where the hell you been?" Buck was smiling again. "Haven't seen or heard from you in months."

"Aw . . . Buck . . . well, I . . . I got a new hobby."

"Hobby? What the hell kind a hobby could you have? Besides being a pervert, that is," Buck laughed.

LaMarr squirmed in his chair. "I've been . . . well, it's kind a different. I . . . I go to funerals," he finally blurted out.

"That's a *hobby?*"

"Hey, Buck, it's not as crazy as you think. I check the obits and go to the interesting ones."

"Interesting funerals! Jesus Christ almighty!"

"You oughta try it, Buck. No kidding. I went to a nudist's funeral the other day. God it was great! *Had* to strip down to get in. It was for a gal about twenty-five. Should have been there, Buck. What a body—the most beautiful boobs you . . ."

"Goddamn you, LaMarr. No more. No more. I swear you're over the goddamn hill."

"Well, you asked," smirked the ex-cop. "Now, whattaya want

50

with me? You still owe me for that last escapade. The little bit of money you gave me barely covered the cost of the flag."

Six months earlier, Buck hired LaMarr to have a flag made and hung over the entrance to the Sacramento, D.C., ACLU Swim and Tennis Club clubhouse. The flag had fifty white stars in a blue field like the American flag, but in place of the stripes was a bright red field with a gold hammer and sickle in the center. When it was discovered, the club members held an emergency meeting. After a short discussion, they voted to keep the flag but remove it from the entrance and hang it from the middle of the ceiling in the formal dining room.

"No problem, LaMarr. Just send me a bill and I'll square it away."

"I've sent six bills already, Buck. You know how much you owe me. Just pay up."

"Okay, LaMarr, okay. You'll get your ten bucks when you leave. But this time I've got a big job for you. It's going to take some bucks to get it done, but I'll sell my house if I have to pay for it."

"If it's that big, Buck, I want my money out front." LaMarr was composed again and grinning from ear to ear.

"Don't sweat it, LaMarr," Buck offered. "You want money, I'll give you a pocket full of cash when you leave." Buck ran down the news about Penny, Wanda Flagella, and Axel Rodd and how they were going to try to blast him in the *Bunion*. "I want you to follow that cunt Penny and bug her house and every place she takes a shit. She's got a dildo she calls Wanda. Get it when you bug the house. And I want you to follow that faggot governor I've got to catch him dirty. I've gotta get those assholes before they get me. And besides, I'm gonna run for governor and beat that little wimp."

"That's a tall order, Buck," mused LaMarr.

51

"You got twelve days. I've got to have some shit on that broad before she comes in to see me."

"That shouldn't be much of a problem, Buck. Not if you got the cash. I'll need some help, and that takes cash money."

Buck walked to his closet, removed an envelope from a floor safe, and handed it to LaMarr. LaMarr quickly thumbed through the stack of twenty-dollar bills. "One thousand dollars. You expect me to bug that dame's house and follow her and that governor all over the state for two weeks on one thousand measly, fuckin' dollars?"

"All right, LaMarr," sighed Buck, resigned. He produced another envelope, which contained another thousand dollars.

"That's still not enough," snickered LaMarr. Buck Mullins was a big, mean man with a badge who didn't much cotton to flashers and faggots and now he stared through LaMarr's perverted skull. "But it'll get me started, Buck," LaMarr offered, heading for the door.

"Thanks, LaMarr. And don't you worry. I'll take real good care of you."

"Sure you will, Buck. I truly do believe that." LaMarr slipped on his trench coat and walked out the door.

Two days later, LaMarr called to report his progress. "Everything is in and operating, Buck. And we got a big bonus. That nut Penny is going to go see some psychiatrist—Hubert Pickthorn-Henriksen—and I'll have the bug in before her first visit. Plus I got that plastic piston she calls Wanda."

"All right, LaMarr! That's good goddamned work!" Buck smiled and stared at his plaques, then at the saddle. "Wrap Wanda up real good and see that she gets delivered to me personally."

"I'll deliver Wanda to you personally, Buck, and when I do, I want another thousand."

"Another thousand! Already? Don't try to bleed me, LaMarr."

"I'm not bleeding you, Buck," LaMarr yelled back. "I gotta pay for a lot of shit, and when I start chasin' the *gay one* around the state, I'll end up owning half of the airlines."

"Okay, okay," conceded Buck. "You'll get the cash when you deliver Wanda."

CHAPTER 7

PENNY PENNY was not just pretty, she was an astonishingly beautiful woman. And her body was perfectly proportioned, much like that of Judee Rose, except that Penny had a *pair* of well-developed breasts. She was also exceedingly intelligent, though her brain blasted away like a sawed-off shotgun and she dressed like a collision of Navajo squaw and San Francisco hippie.

Penny was born and raised in Sacramento and attended local Catholic girls' schools, but she matriculated and more at U.C. Berkeley, where she was *born again again*. She managed to preserve her virginity for one semester. However, at the urging of her counselor, she then enrolled in Introduction to Sexual Awareness, a class that explored all aspects of sexual behavior. Penny became so enamored of both the lab work and homework that her virginity soon became a vague and rather silly memory, a tattered flag fluttering in the breeze of new awareness. Scoring virtually at will in all sexual sports, Penny moved through the advanced classes and a giddy succession of partners—both male and female—until she met Wanda Flagella. In Advanced Sexual

Awareness the beautiful Penny was always in demand as a lab partner. She had her choice and in the end picked Wanda, who was so ugly that she never got past the autoerotic portion of lab until the compassionate Penny came along. They did their homework together and were soon inseparable, though Penny continued to have her little *problem*—men and their particular brand of organ music. At the suggestion of a psychiatrist, Wanda bought *Little Wanda*, hand-painted it in art class and presented it to Penny on her birthday. It must have done the trick because Penny and Wanda had been together ever since.

Upon finishing college, Penny worked for local newspapers in Berkeley while Wanda went to law school. After she graduated, they moved to Sacramento, D.C., where Wanda started a law practice, running a local American Civil Liberties Union office, and Penny went to work for the *Bunion*. J.J. had befriended the pair when he and Wanda were classmates in law school.

Although Penny joined many causes while attending college, it was the one she organized herself that almost got her killed. It was called OR (for One Race). The object of the drive was to get a law passed that would ban caucasians from marrying caucasians and require they marry only members of an ethnic minority race. It got off to a good start but soon after the initial publicity, she began receiving death threats, openly, from large ethnic minority organizations. It was made quite clear that minorities didn't want to be forced into marrying whites. Penny saw the error of her ways and folded up her tent.

To Penny, life's beauty was to be found in human involvements, not physical appearances. This philosophy became readily apparent with one glance at Wanda, who though very intelligent looked slightly retarded. With her eyelids drooping and her mouth always half open, Wanda always seemed on the verge of falling into a catatonic trance. She was chunky and of medium height, with faded blue eyes and a pale complexion never enhanced by makeup, chopped-off brown hair, a small mound of fat between her shoulder blades, and overly fond of mumu-style dresses. And Penny, strangely enough, was both oblivious to Wanda's ugliness and equally unaware of her own beauty. It just was not important.

What was important to Penny were pretty relationships—human involvements unfettered by emotional frustrations—and this beauty and beast had enjoyed such a relationship right up to the moment when Axel Rodd had so unceremoniously emptied her purse and Little Wanda clattered out on his desk. Now she would have to give up Little Wanda, at least have to give up carrying her in her purse. Foreboding dark clouds, shaped like men, began to form on Penny's horizon.

Penny and Wanda shared apartments for many years before having a home built in the foothills to the northeast of Sacramento, D.C., where their closest neighbor was a quarter mile away. Over the front entrance they hung a sign that said Cuddle Cove. The large home had all the modern conveniences, as well as an outdoor pool and an enormous playroom designed by Wanda.

The playroom featured a large, sunken, Roman-style pool in its center, with alternating, underwater lights that constantly changed the color of the circulating water. Surrounding the pool were body-length overstuffed cushions of various bright colors. The room also contained three king-size waterbeds, primarily used by partying guests, but Wanda's favorite part, appropriately called Wanda's Corner, featured a conventional king-size bed with built-in restraining straps designed by a Berkeley professor. Hanging from wall pegs were more straps, conventional cotton ropes, braided cashmere ropes and whips, several silver- and gold-colored link chains made of soft rubber, and three pairs of gold-plated handcuffs.

The activities that took place in this room were of course very personal and to even hint at what might have occurred would be a serious invasion of their right to privacy.

After arranging the interview with Buck, Penny felt pretty good, having temporarily forgotten about Little Wanda. But half-way to Cuddle Cove, the foreboding clouds again appeared, and by the time she reached home, her frustrations were obvious. Wanda, however, had problems of her own: her mouth hung agape, and her eyes were almost closed.

"Oh, Wanda, dear, what is the matter?" asked Penny, letting her own problems slide to the back of her mind.

Wanda opened her eyes slightly. "Nothing earthshaking, dear. It's just that the cases we're now getting are very frustrating. Very difficult to make a decision when you must consider the political implications."

"Not that one about letting the police talk to *innocent* people who they think committed a crime. You're not going to let them do that, are you Wanda?"

"Oh, no, no," Wanda assured her. "That will *never* be allowed again in this state. If a cop so much as says *hello* to a suspect, the case will be thrown out. No more so-called voluntary confessions. They're grossly unconstitutional. The vote was unanimous, and our decision will be released next week."

"That's wonderful, Wanda, but that should have made you very happy."

"Oh, it did," replied the chief justice. "It did! After I polled the justices, we all went to the ACLU Swim and Tennis Club for a bowl of borscht and a belt of vodka to celebrate. Had a great time.

"No, it's the People versus Anne Whitlow that's causing so much frustration," Wanda explained. "She's the convicted prostitute who's alleging that her constitutional rights were violated when she was ordered and forced to stand trial. In the brief filed with the court her counsel points out, and rightly so, that if a person is considered innocent, it would be a violation of her constitutional rights to force her to stand trial against her free will."

"Well, that sounds logical to me," Penny said, a look of wonderment spreading across her face. "That should be an easy enough decision to make."

"Think about it, Penny," Wanda moaned. "What would happen if people quit volunteering to go on trial? Judges and probation officers and public defenders would lose their jobs. Lawyers practicing criminal law would go broke. And worse yet, the ACLU and National Lawyers Guild would probably fold. No, Penny dear, the tragic consequences dictate that I put politics and economics above principle in this case." Tears began to well up in her eyes.

"Oh, Wanda," Penny sympathized. "It will be all right. Time heals all wounds," she said reassuringly.

They walked hand in hand into their lavishly furnished living room, then separated, taking different chairs. They sat in silence for a full half hour, Wanda focused on the complexities of her office, while Penny's scattershot mind found many different targets—the confrontation with Axel, the disquieting thoughts of men, the manuscript that Wanda didn't know about.

The manuscript. In college Penny had written a novel based

on her sexual fantasies about men. She had packed the finished manuscript away, and Wanda had never seen it. But it was hot—hotter than Tabasco sauce in an open wound—and as she thought about it now, a new fire for men began to kindle in Penny's mind, causing her to feel at once promiscuous and guilty for this "adulterous" act. Passion and shame flushed her face, and Wanda noticed the sudden surge of color.

"Penny, dear, what is the matter? Sitting here feeling sorry for myself, I've just come to notice the pain in your beautiful face."

"Oh, Wanda," Penny cried. "It's Axel."

"What did that dreadful man do now?"

"It was terrible," Penny said, tears washing over her sculpted cheekbones. "He called me into his office, took my purse, and dumped Little Wanda out on his desk, right in front of Stoney Gilson. Then he ordered me to take her home and burn her. Oh, darling, I can't burn Little Wanda, and I won't be able to take her with me anymore. I'm already starting to have *impure* thoughts."

"Stoney Gilson saw Little Wanda?" Wanda was shaken. "That Axel Rodd is a bilge rat. If I didn't have such a good job, we'd move out of this town. They ought to move the court back to San Francisco, where it belongs. I could kill J.J. for moving everything to his wonderful Sacramento, D.C."

"It's all right, Wanda," Penny assured her. "Stoney won't say anything. Axel thinks he'll tell Sheriff Mullins, but I don't think so. I'll hide Little Wanda here."

"That's not the main problem," Wanda moaned. "What about you? What about us? You know what happens when you think about men. You know what that does to our relationship! I can't stand the thought of you thinking about men!"

"I know, I know, Wanda," Penny pleaded, "but what can we do?"

"You'll have to see a psychiatrist," Wanda said. Her voice was kind but firm.

"A psychiatrist!" Penny screamed. Then she began sobbing again. "I'm not crazy. It's that damn Axel's fault."

"Oh, Penny, I know you're not crazy," Wanda sympathized. "But maybe a good psychiatrist could recommend something to replace Little Wanda."

"Do you really think so? I hope you're right, Wanda. We have to do something," Penny cried. "But I don't know of any psychiatrists. Not one that I would trust anyway."

"Well, I read about that Dr. Wilson W. Wilson in the paper," Wanda offered. "He's supposed to be a nationally known expert, but he looks too straight." They sat for a moment in silence, staring at the floor, before Wanda continued. "I do know of this one guy—Dr. Hubert Pickthorn-Henriksen. He's probably straight and a little goofy, but he specializes in female emotional problems. Let's give him a try. If that doesn't work, we'll go somewhere else."

"Wonderful!" exclaimed Penny. "I feel better already."

Two days later Penny had an appointment with Doctor Pickthorn-Henriksen for the following week, their house was expertly bugged, and Little Wanda's batteries were expiring in Sheriff Buck Mullins' safe.

CHAPTER 8

CONTRARY TO HIS POLITICAL philosophy, J.J. was a conservative in terms of dress. He always wore either a gray or dark blue suit, freshly cleaned and pressed, with a blue or white shirt and conservative tie. However, he required that his suits and shirts go through an aging process before he would wear them. New suits were worn by an assistant for three to five months before being passed on to J.J. New shirts were laundered a dozen times or more and sun dried between washings. Then portions of the collar and cuffs were carefully sanded with emery cloth to achieve that just-about-frayed look. J.J. kept none of these clothes. His closet was empty, much like the rest of his apartment. Every morning, however, the clothes that he would need for the day were laid out and waiting for him. The same thing occurred whenever and wherever he traveled. J.J. never packed a suitcase.

The man responsible for this was Sammi Bamboozi. Although he was officially the Special Assistant to the Governor for State Beautification and Cultural Affairs and drew a healthy salary, Sammi was actually J.J.'s personal gofer. He anticipated all of

J.J.'s needs, and all his needs were met in turn. Sammi was the only person privy to almost every aspect of J.J.'s personal life and traveled with him everywhere. Well, almost everywhere. There were a few things that even Sammi didn't know. It was when Stoney Gilson contacted Sammi Bamboozi that J.J. became irate and had his chief of staff, Red Ainess, talk to Axel Rodd. Sammi of course would not utter so much as a grunt in response to many of Stoney's questions. In fact he would not even acknowledge that he knew the governor. "I don't know what you talk about. What you want for Chris' sake!"

On the morning of the big press conference on color TV, Sammi had provided a medium-gray suit, light blue shirt, and blue striped tie. J.J. awakened feeling good. After a shower and shave, he dressed and drank a glass of cold orange juice (the sole contents of his refrigerator). His capitol office was only a quarter mile away, and during the summer J.J. usually rode to work on his Vespa, but on this beautiful cool morning he decided to walk. This was promptly leaked to the press, and J.J. was soon joined by a phalanx of reporters and photographers, who were chatting and snapping pictures.

J.J. went straight to his office, advising his entourage that he would see them again momentarily in the press conference room, more commonly known as the Arena. Normally J.J. would have remained with the reporters and casually walked into the press room, but today was special, and he wanted the room filled, with everyone in their seats and properly warmed up, before he made his entrance. The combination of advanced notices and well-orchestrated leaks had duly hyped the press corps for this momentous event.

The room was filled to standing-room-only capacity. Dozens of microphones were taped and stacked on the lectern, and the TV cameramen and still photographers jostled with the print media for prime locations. In the front row sat the crewcut reporter representing the *San Francisco Examiner,* smoking a small cigar. He was built like Tarzan but had a voice like Jane. He was also wearing lipstick, a bright yellow dress with matching handbag, and splashy gold earrings. Several of J.J.'s aides stood against the walls at various points throughout the room to provide a semblance of security as well as lead the applause.

Red Ainess, at the lectern to introduce the governor, was startled to see Stoney Gilson enter the Arena. Stoney looked around, acknowledged Ainess with a malicious smile, and seated himself near the center rear of the room, looking down on the lectern from the gradually elevated seats. Stoney was as much an anomaly here as he was at the *Bunion.* Although there were press people here from all over the country, they all looked alike—sloppy in dress and crude in manner. If they didn't like you they played the shark; if they did, they all asked the same benign questions, leaving your dignity and reputation very much intact. This particular gathering liked J.J. so much that any member who stepped out of line would be immediately stoned to death. Stoney knew this but would not allow it to affect his decisions, whichever way he decided to go.

After a few perfunctory remarks, Red Ainess introduced J.J., who entered from stage left to a standing ovation and took his place at the lectern. He stood smiling for a minute, acknowledging several reporters in the audience. "Thank you, ladies and gentlemen, thank you," he said, still smiling, waving his right hand slightly above his shoulder. "You are indeed so kind and such a pleasure to be with. I only wish that we could get together more often."

Though J.J.'s conservative attire and natty appearance gave the impression that he was a stickler for detail and propriety, his oratory was decidedly casual. This normally incongruous combination was no accident. It was developed by J.J. and his staff, who referred to it in private as incidental orderliness. J.J.'s appeal was almost universal among the various political disciplines. To the conservatives, he didn't *look* like a liberal, and to the liberals, he didn't *sound* like a conservative.

"My friends," J.J. went on, "I have two very important bits of news for you today, but I want to save the best for last. So if you don't mind, I'll take your questions first, whatever is on your mind. Then we'll get on to what I have in mind for the people of this great state." Hands immediately shot up, and J.J. recognized a reporter sitting in the front row.

"Thank you, Governor," the reporter began. "My question has to do with your future. Since it is more or less a foregone conclusion that you will be reelected next year, and with the president announcing he will not run again, are you seriously considering seeking the Democratic presidential nomination two years from now?"

A round of applause, starting from the walls in, indicated overwhelming approval for a positive response.

J.J., smiling, both hands raised, palms out, waving, signaled for quiet. "Thank you for the spontaneous indication of support, but to answer your question, I feel it premature to make such an important decision at this time. I'm running for reelection to this humble office, not the presidency, and I have to prepare for opposition, however token that opposition may be. And if the rumors I'm hearing are true, my opposition will be just that— *token!*" J.J. laughed. The audience roared.

Red Ainess looked like he just sat down on a cattle prod. He knew that J.J.'s statement would be well publicized and would only cause Buck to come back swinging and digging all the harder.

Keep it up, J.J., thought Stoney, and that crazy Okie sheriff will have such a posse on you that you'll never have another private moment in your life. Stoney blew Red Ainess a kiss.

J.J., wishing to acknowledge the reporter who asked the first question, said, "Thank you for the excellent question."

"The byline's Sally," said the man in the yellow dress as he toyed with one of his gold earrings. "I'm with the *San Francisco Examiner.*"

"Well, thanks for being with us today," J.J. said, pointing to another raised hand.

"Yes, Governor. Asa Johnson with the *Loomis Daily Herald*," said the grizzled black man as he rose to his feet. "There is now a major rift between the mushroom farmers and the California Mushroom Production Control Commission. What, if anything, can be done about it?"

"Well, by law, not very much," J.J. responded quickly. "That commission is under the control of the lieutenant governor, so you'll have to direct your question to that office."

Asa Johnson was puzzled. "Lieutenant governor? Governor," he asked, "who is the lieutenant governor?"

"Well, Mr. Johnson, you know it just dawned on me that we don't *have* one. Got left off the ballot in the last election and I guess no one noticed till now. I'll have to look into that and see if we can get one appointed or something to look into that mushroom problem." J.J. smiled and pointed to a pretty young Asian woman. He was covering all the bases.

"Yes, Governor," she said, dropping her hand and remaining seated. "I have it from an informed source that the state intends to *nationalize* or purchase Palm Springs. Could this have anything to do with your Reverse Punishment Crime Control Master Plan?"

"Well, I was not aware that the Palm Springs plan was a

matter of public record," acknowledged J.J. with a chuckle. "That's one leak I didn't know about." Laughter all around. When it subsided, J.J. continued.

"As most of you are aware, when I took office, we implemented my Reverse Punishment Crime Control Program. We tore down all those ghastly prisons and purchased or obtained through condemnation proceedings country clubs, hotels, and resorts throughout the state, turning them into Reverse Punishment Crime Control Colonies. And as we knew they would, people by the droves began turning themselves in, alleging that they had committed various felonies. Those who could prove that they had in fact committed a felony were admitted to one of the colonies. The prosecutors became public defenders, trying to keep them out, while the public defenders became prosecutors, trying to get their clients in." J.J. smiled and looked about the room, measuring the expressions on the various reporters' faces.

"Though it was an immediate success," he continued, "the real meat of the program came later when the colonies began to fill up and the waiting lists began to grow. The crime rate, which increased sharply in the beginning, began to fall to the point where we now have a very negative crime index."

"But Governor," the Asian beauty interjected, "if Palm Springs becomes a Reverse Punishment Crime Control Colony, more space will open up, the lines will dwindle, and people will start committing crimes again."

"But that's the whole point—the genius of this program— the control of crime both up and down," said the governor. "We must realize and accept that crime and the criminal are a viable part of our economy. A totally negative crime index would eventually seriously impact our entire economy. Why, judges, lawyers, guards, probation officers, and beat cops, just to name a few, would lose their jobs. Lock and alarm companies would fold. Insurance companies would go under. We'd have to abolish our wonderful Victim of Violent Crime Assistance Program for lack of victims. But that can never happen with this all-encompassing program, and so our economy will continue to flourish."

"Thank you, Governor, for that explanation," responded the female reporter. Then she bowed slightly and said, "You are to be commended for your wisdom."

"Why, thank you!" exclaimed J.J., flashing his porcelain. He bowed slightly himself in the direction of the Asian and said, "You honor me."

Stoney had come to the conference intending to take notes and file his story, without incident, but he could hold back no longer. Knowing that he would never be called on, he didn't bother to raise his hand for recognition. He fired his question as he came to his feet. "Governor, Stoney Gilson of the *Sacramento Bunion*. Governor, following your reasoning to its logical conclusion means that the entire state will eventually become a Reverse Punishment Crime Control Colony. Have you developed contingency plans to prevent this from happening?"

"Thank you, Mr. Gilson," J.J. said, still smiling. "An excellent comment, and I agree with you one hundred percent. The answer to your question is yes. We have explored every contingency. Next question."

"Wait, hold it!" yelled Stoney. "That's no answer."

"I think it is, Mr. Gilson," J.J. said calmly, still smiling. "I think we should do it. I'm all for it."

"Do what, Governor? That was *my* question!"

"We have a plan to do exactly what you suggested. It's obviously what the people want. Now, please, Mr. Gilson," J.J. pleaded, "do sit down."

"But I didn't suggest any . . . ," Stoney's voice trailed off. "Darn! I don't believe it," he mumbled to himself as he sat down to a mixed chorus of hisses and boos, and applause for J.J.

J.J., happy with the way in which he had disposed of Stoney Gilson, announced that the question-and-answer period was over. It was time for the main event. "Ladies and gentlemen, it's time to let you know the purpose for which we are gathered here today. You will indeed take part in a great historical event, and I can't think of a finer group of people that I would care to share this momentous occasion with.

"Mr. Ainess will be passing out copies of the two documents I hold in my hand. While they are being distributed, I will be signing the originals, making their contents official. At the end of the conference, we'll hold a drawing for the pens that I use, so don't run off."

As Red Ainess began his chore, J.J. moved to a table with a rack of pens before him to begin signing the two executive orders. Photographers immediately clamored for positions around the table to film and photograph the historic moment.

As the reporters read the documents and began to fully comprehend their historical impact, a roar of excited conversation filled the conference room. Some clapped their hands, some cheered, others clapped their hands and cheered, and Stoney Gilson did neither. He simply sat, staring at the documents in disbelief.

State of California
Office of the Governor
Sacramento, D.C.
Executive Order Number 306

To the members of the California State Legislature and the people of the Great State of California, greetings:

1. By the power vested in me by the Constitution of the Great State of California, as the Chief Executive Officer, I hereby declare that the Native Californian is an endangered species and that a State of Emergency does exist.

2. For the purposes of this order, all legal residents of the State, upon the signing of this order, will be considered Native Californians and will be granted citizenship.

3. Those who decline citizenship will be required to remove themselves from the State within a period of ten (10) days from the date of the signing of this order.

4. Those noncitizens who wish to visit this State must possess a valid passport, beginning ten (10) days after the signing of this order.

5. Those noncitizens who wish to visit or remain in this State for a period exceeding fourteen (14) days must obtain a visa.

6. Nothing in this order shall pertain to members of the news media who possess a valid press credential issued by my office and are citizens of the United States of America.

SEAL   Signed _____

                      Harry Hamilton Baal III

           Dated _____

71

State of California
Office of the Governor
Sacramento, D.C.
Executive Order Number 307

To the members of the California State Legislature and the people of the Great State of California, greetings:

Whereas the Governor of the Great State of California, by the issuance of Executive Order Number 306, declared the Native Californian to be an endangered species and further declared a State of Emergency, this order is issued as an emergency response to the emergency in order to protect the endangered species.

1. Upon the signing of this order, a double cyclone fence, fifteen (15) feet high, shall be constructed on the terrestrial perimeter of this State, within one hundred (100) feet of the legal boundaries of this State and the adjoining states.

2. The California National Guard shall be deployed to patrol the terrestrial boundary fence, and from this day forward the fence shall be referred to as the Great Wall of California.

3. A California Coast Guard shall be established and deployed to patrol all waters within thirty (30) miles of the State terrestrial boundary ending at the Pacific Ocean.

4. All islands within the above stated thirty (30) mile limit shall remain under the control of the Great State of California.

SEAL   Signed _____
                      Harry Hamilton Baal III

            Dated _____

After signing Executive Order Number 307, J.J. moved back to the lectern. "Ladies and gentlemen," he bellowed, again commanding the attention of those gathered in the hall. "Ladies and gentlemen, I know that you're very excited, as I am, and I appreciate your enthusiasm. This is indeed a great day for the people of this great state!" J.J. raised his hands high in the air, his fingers forming victory signs, and the audience roared with approval.

It would be more appropriate if his middle fingers were pointing to the sky, Stoney thought to himself.

"I know that these exciting documents speak for themselves," J.J. continued, "but if anyone has a question. Yes sir, you in the back row."

"Yes, Governor. Jerry Green, with the World Wide Press International wire services. Mr. Governor, when will this fence, or I should say Great Wall, be constructed?"

"Construction has begun!" J.J. exclaimed. "At the moment my pen touched Executive Order Number 307, a message was sent to the border and the first posthole was dug." Another roar of approval echoed through the room.

"Governor," said a young female reporter, "a fence is not the most attractive thing to view. What will be done to beautify this great monument?"

"Good question," J.J. said. "The cyclone fence structure is only temporary. Mr. Bamboozi, my special assistant for State Beautification and Cultural Affairs, is working on architectural plans for a rock structure that will put that mess in China to shame." Laughter and applause.

"Mr. Governor, Harold Blue of the *Washington Rail*. Mr. Governor, may we assume that the communications satellite you launched several months ago had something to do with the events that took place here today?"

"Yes, you may," admitted J.J. "In fact it is a spy satellite that will help us keep an eye on places like Washington, D.C., New York, Chicago, and Detroit, just to name a few. It will also be of assistance in controlling our border and coastline."

"Mr. Governor," said a serious young man, rising to his feet. "Mr. Governor, what if Congress attempts to take action—legal or otherwise—against the Great Wall. What are you prepared to do?"

"The Great Wall will be well within our sovereign state boundary, young man. Should the Congress or chief executive take *any* action against it, we would consider that an act of aggression, an act of war, and we would respond accordingly.

"Okay. Just one more question," J.J. said, pointing to Sally in the front row.

"Thank you, Governor," he squeaked. "If you should run for president and be elected, what will be your attitude toward Washington, D.C.?"

J.J. stared at Sally for a moment. "I have to admit—Sally, isn't it?—that I would very strongly consider closing the place down entirely! Thank you, ladies and gentlemen," he said, laughing as he started to leave the lectern.

"Wait. Wait, please, Mr. Governor!" The gorgeous blonde was practically having a fit. "Please, just one more question."

J.J. paused briefly and then returned to the lectern. "Fire away, miss, and this *is* the last one."

"Mr. Governor," she proceeded, "would you comment on the rumors concerning your romantic involvement with Miss Antoinette Mandrocci?"

Boy, that's a plant if I ever saw one, thought Stoney.

"Miss Mandrocci?" A mischievous grin appeared on J.J.'s face.

"Oh, come on, J.J., watch the overkill," Stoney mumbled.

"Come now, Governor," purred the blonde, smiling affectionately. "We know that she's arriving at the airport at this very moment, to visit you."

J.J. straightened his spine and stiffened his jaw. "Well, Miss, on a day of such historical moment for the state of California, I hardly feel it appropriate to either confirm or deny rumors. If I must say something, let me just say that we're good friends who enjoy each other's company. We'll visit for a couple of days and share the supper table, but I can assure you that everything will be quite proper!" J.J. smiled and left the lectern with a wave to the reporters.

Stoney didn't stay to see if he'd won a pen at the drawing. He filed his story without comment and without talking to Axel, then began preparations for his trip to Mobile.

CHAPTER 9

WHEN ANTOINETTE "TONI" MANDROCCI boarded her plane in Mobile, she was relieved to be leaving the intense humidity of Alabama for the more bearable, dry heat of Sacramento, D.C. She was also looking forward to a quiet three days with J.J., unlike their last visit, when they were hounded by reporters and photographers at every turn. Toni was twenty-seven, fourteen years younger than her brother Georgie, who was the same age as J.J. She had known J.J. most of her life but had never thought of him as a possible suitor, so his sudden invitation for their first visit nearly two months earlier came as something of a surprise. She enjoyed the handsome, wealthy young governor very much, but the accompanying press and the attendant publicity made her extremely edgy. Though Toni was a model and came from a political family and so was very much attuned to public life, uninvited invasions of her privacy were normally met with uncontrolled hostility.

Toni and Georgie were born and raised in Prichard, Alabama, where their father, Percy, was a wealthy businessman and mayor of the city. Like Georgie, Toni attended the University of Alabama at Tuscaloosa; unlike Georgie, however, Toni didn't stick around for graduation. Her five feet seven inches, black hair, deep brown eyes, pretty face with full pouty lips, and exquisite figure added up to the Miss Alabama title in her sophomore year. More than just a piece of assets, Toni was also smart—smart enough to realize that modeling might be much more interesting and would definitely be much more lucrative than teaching elementary school. She wasn't wrong.

J.J. knew that Toni had been of great value to Georgie in his successful congressional campaigns, and with that in mind he had asked Georgie to help set up their first "date." Georgie was always happy to help J.J., and when Toni received the call from J.J. two days later, she was both curious and excited to accept his invitation.

That first date had turned out to be painfully public, and although J.J. was very convincing in his explanation about the press and publicity, Toni remained apprehensive when her plane touched down at the Sacramento, D.C., International Airport. When she entered the passenger disembarkation area to a flood of reporters and photographers, her fears were confirmed. She kept her wide smile but blew up inside.

As he had the first time, Sammi Bamboozi—a short, chunky man with short-cropped, black kinky hair and a bald spot beginning to form toward the back of his head—was there to meet her. Sammi had a constantly worried look that he continually covered with a nervous flash of a smile. His suits were always in some disarray and disrepair and his shoes always a bit short of a shine.

Before Sammi could get to Toni, an overflow crowd of newspeople surrounded her, screaming questions, churning tape, and clicking cameras.

78

"Toni! Hey, Toni! How serious is it?" one reporter yelled. "Have you set a date yet?"

"What do those Rebs think about your dating a *Yankee?*" screamed another.

A grinning idiot, directly in front of her, smirked, "Is the Guv a good love, Miss Mandrocci?"

One look at Toni's sickly, pasted-on smile made Sammi's stomach begin to churn, and at his signal, three burly young men bore their way through the mob and rescued her from the make-shift arena. As they darted for the waiting car, Sammi held out his hand, which she refused with a smile.

As the car sped away with Toni and Sammi seated in back, Toni dropped the phony smile. Sammi picked it up and flashed three quick ones.

"Now, look here, Mr. Bamboozler!" Toni yelled, pointing a gun-shaped thumb and index finger at his nose.

"Bamboozi, Miss Mandrocci. Bamboozi," he pleaded. Two more quick smiles didn't put her off.

"To me you're a Bamboozler. No. On second thought, you and J.J. are a couple of shitheads. Got that, Bamboozler? A couple of shitheads."

"Please, Miss Mandrocci," Sammi said, raising his right hand in preparation to make a point.

"Why, Mr. Bamboozler," Toni drawled with mock affection, "if you don't do something about your weak wrists, I swear your hands'll fall off someday."

Sammi blushed slightly and lowered his hand. "Please, Miss Mandrocci, let me explain. Neither the governor nor I had any-thing to do with this press fiasco. His orders were that your arrival was to be treated as strictly confidential, and he is going to be mighty upset when he learns of this gross invasion of your pri-vacy." Sammi delivered these lies without taking a breath or flashing one smile. But his assurances seemed to calm Toni, and they continued to the hotel in silence. But when she stepped from the car, the newshounds were lying in ambush.

The first one to reach her was the grinning idiot from the airport. When he opened his mouth, Toni delivered a right cross to the jaw that rattled his teeth and sent him sprawling. As he lay on the ground, she nailed his right hand to the pavement with one of her spike high heels. A photographer moved in to film the action. In one motion Toni whirled and punted his testicles into his throat. As he lay writhing and grabbing his crotch, she grabbed his spanking-new video camera and smashed it into the pavement, shattering the lens and causing the tape to spew out in a curly stream.

A third brave soul moved in, holding his camera with one hand and his crotch with the other. Toni turned on him like a cornered lioness, yanked his camera aside, and thrust her finger into his eye. When he instinctively reached for his throbbing eye, she turned him into a eunuch with the driving force of her right knee.

With that last unmerciful display of inhuman fury, the army of newshounds gathered up their wounded and fled the battleground. As they did so, Toni picked up a broken Leica and hurled it at the grinning idiot. The camera smashed into the back of his head and sent him spinning, first into a phone booth, where his nose splintered, and then into the street, where a honking, squealing taxi nearly put him out of his misery and the driver screamed terrible things about his mother.

Awestruck, Sammi and the three bodyguards never moved from the safety of their seats in the car during the entire one-sided battle. When it was over, they all noticed that they were clutching their crotches.

Toni fluffed her hair, straightened her dress, and walked to the car. "Well, Bamboozler," she said with a victorious smile, "what are you waiting for? Let's get me checked into this dump."

"Yes, Miss Mandrocci," he said, trembling a bit as he stepped from the car. "Right away."

"The south shall rise again," mumbled one of the bodyguards, "if she has anything to do with it."

As they walked into the hotel lobby, the manager addressed her very nervously. "Miss . . . Miss Mandrocci, we . . . welcome you to Sacramento, D.C." He smiled weakly.

Still completely absorbed by the wild skirmish that had just taken place outside his welcome mat, the manager forgot about the contingent of newspeople skulking near Toni's room on the eighteenth floor.

"Why, thank you, sir. You appear to be a real gentleman. Now, if you would be so kind, I've had quite an exhausting trip and would like to enjoy the privacy of my room."

"Of course, Miss Mandrocci. I'll just get a bellboy to show you . . . oh Lord!" he stammered, suddenly remembering what awaited her and envisioning a miniholocaust on the eighteenth floor. "Miss Mandrocci, please. *Please!* Just give me a few minutes. There's one little thing I forgot to prepare." He slapped his forehead. "I promise, it will just take a moment."

Toni sat in the bar with a complimentary glass of Dom Perignon while the manager gathered together his brawniest bellboys, armed them with baseball bats, and sent them up to clear the eighteenth floor. A short time later, a sheepish-looking group of reporters and photographers was herded down the service elevator and out the back door of the hotel.

The rest of the day proceeded quietly. Toni was checked into her suite of rooms, and Sammi graciously, if somewhat nervously, bid her farewell. The three seemingly superfluous bodyguards remained, out of sight, near her room.

Sammi promptly reported the events of the day to J.J., who was elated but anxious. "This will get us more press than we could ever have hoped for—probably worldwide," said the governor. But he knew when he said it that his days of playing games with Toni were over. He could probably ride this one out, but future publicity concerning his "romance" with Toni would require a new plan.

J.J. arrived at the hotel promptly at 8 P.M., fully expecting a crush of newspeople—his itinerary having been properly leaked— but other than a few guests roaming about the lobby and a few more drinking and chattering in the bar, the place was dead. J.J. scanned the rooftops surrounding the hotel and found them vacant. She must have really done a job on those guys, he thought to himself.

He nodded to the night manager and clerks as he walked to the elevator, and they all waved back or grinned or giggled with recognition. The ride to the eighteenth floor seemed awfully slow, and by the time he exited the elevator, J.J. was slightly stiff with apprehension.

The black-haired beauty who opened the door was dressed for something other than dinner. Toni's full-length, white night-gown wasn't transparent but was sheer enough that J.J. could tell she was naked underneath. He stiffened a little more.

"J.J., honey, come on in," Toni drawled sweetly. Then she closed and locked the door behind him.

J.J. walked to the center of the small living room, looked about, and turned to her. "Very nice, very nice. I approve. How was your trip? Any problems?"

"Problems?" Toni put her arms around his neck and rubbed up against him. "J.J., darling, problems are those little ol' things a person doesn't know how to take care of. I don't have any problems." She pulled his head down and planted her lips on his, smearing lipstick on his face. "Welcome to my suite, my sweet!"

J.J., taken by surprise, pulled back nervously. He yanked the handkerchief from his breast pocket and dabbed at the lipstick. "Toni, you should be getting ready. We have to go out." J.J. noticed that his hand was shaking slightly. He put down the handkerchief and continued. "I have a room reserved for a small, *private* cocktail party at the ACLU Swim and Tennis Club. Then we'll go to Old Sacramento, D.C., for a nice, *private* dinner for two."

"No, honey," Toni said with a mischievous smile, "we're going to have a nice private dinner right here. And I *am* dressed for it."

"But Toni," J.J. stammered.

Toni put her finger on his lips to shush him. "Now, J.J., I've already ordered our dinner from room service. You're having a double order of raw oysters on the half shell. They're *so* good for you," she purred. "Then we'll have just a little champagne. Not too much. That could ruin a delightful evening."

J.J. managed to choke down his oysters with a smile. As they ate and, afterward, as they sipped French champagne, they discussed their future. Toni decreed that future visits would take place in Alabama, away from the press and without advance notice. J.J. reluctantly agreed, while thinking to himself that news of their meetings could be leaked after the fact—secret rendezvous made excellent press. Actually, he liked that even better.

When the time came, J.J. managed a satisfactory sexual performance, as visions of Tarzan and Superman danced in his head.

On her flight back to Mobile, Toni smiled giddily, unaware that she was entitled to hang a gold-plated cherry over the mantel of her fireplace.

CHAPTER 10

WHEN THE DAY OF HER appointment with Dr. Hubert Pick-thorn-Henriksen arrived, Penny was feeling good. She hadn't missed Little Wanda all that much, and as far as she was concerned, it was still safely hidden away. She felt confident that a substitute would be found. But some minor, almost imperceptible changes were taking place. For one, she was wearing a little more makeup, though she was not consciously aware of this. Wanda was, but she was not alarmed; in fact she rather liked it. Penny did feel a slight magnetism toward men, but she knew that this "problem" would be resolved.

As she parked her car Penny was amazed at the size of the Pickthorn-Henriksen Medical Complex office building and the little inpatient cottages scattered about the manicured grounds. The professional atmosphere of the outside changed abruptly when she entered Dr. Pickthorn-Henriksen's office. The flocked wallpaper and furnishings reminded Penny of the front room of a French bordello, even though she had never been in a French bordello. Her novel was tucked under her arm like a sheltered puppy.

An attractive lady sat at the desk in the dimly lit office. Her nameplate indicated that she was a registered nurse. Other than Penny, she was the only person present. As Penny approached, the nurse looked up and smiled. "Good morning, you must be Miss Penny Penny. Welcome to the Hubert Pickthorn-Henriksen Treatment Center. My name is Miss Pamela Aphrodyte, but you may call me Pam. I'm the doctor's personal secretary and attending nurse. I know you're going to enjoy your stay here." She smiled again.

"My stay?"

"Well, I guess that was a bit presumptuous of me," chuckled Nurse Aphrodyte. "You see, after their initial therapy session, many of our patients choose to stay on for more intensive treatment—by the doctor or one of his expert associates. But, please don't decide until the end of the day."

"End of the day?"

"Oh, yes," chirped the nurse. "The doctor takes such a personal interest in all of his patients that his initial examination and therapy session can be quite extensive and involved."

Penny just stared at the nurse, not quite comprehending. The nurse continued. "Now please fill these papers out completely," she said, handing Penny a stack of forms. "You can use the desk at the other end of the room."

Two hours later, Penny had answered all the questions, explained in detail the reasons for her visit, and returned the completed forms to Nurse Aphrodyte.

"Thank you, Penny. Please have a seat while I run these in to the doctor." She returned a few moments later. "Now, Miss Penny, I will need a check for five hundred dollars or your insurance policy number to cover the initial visit and consultation."

"Five hundred dollars!" cried Penny. "For the first visit?"

"It's well worth it," assured the nurse, "and that's the maximum that the insurance will pay."

"Well, okay, but I prefer to handle this privately." She took her checkbook out of her purse, made out the check, and handed it to Nurse Aphrodyte.

"Thank you, Penny," she said, clutching the check. "The doctor won't be too long now."

Twenty minutes later the nurse escorted Penny into Dr. Hubert Pickthorn-Henriksen's office.

The doctor was five feet eight and somewhat emaciated, with a short trunk and very long legs. If the rest of his body had grown in proportion to his legs, he would have been at least six inches taller. He had a bright red crewcut and pale blue eyes, and always walked with one stiff leg. Sometimes it was the right leg, sometimes the left. When Penny appeared at the door, he stood up from his desk.

"Have a seat, my dear," he said in a comforting way as he motioned to a chair in front of his desk.

"Thank you, doctor," Penny said nervously as she tried to read his credentials from the framed certificates hanging on one wall.

"Relax, Miss Penny. I've read your file thoroughly, and I have no doubts whatsoever that we'll be able to help you."

"Oh, that's wonderful," she sighed. "I hope it doesn't take too long—too many sessions, I mean."

"Well," the doctor paused and smiled, "that will be strictly up to you, my dear. Now, Penny, let's begin. Please stand, walk to the corner there, and turn slowly for me a couple of times."

Penny seemed confused but complied, while the doctor eyed her up and down. "What's the purpose of this?" she asked, somewhat bewildered.

"Well, my dear," he said, fingering his stethoscope, "I have to give you a physical examination, and I charge according to the shape of the body, by the pound. How much do you weigh?"

"One twenty-six," she answered automatically, without thinking. "By the pound! You charge by the pound?"

"Why, yes," he answered, as if that were perfectly natural. "For a very grotesque body, I charge up to five dollars per pound. For you, the minimum. Fifty cents a pound. Sixty-three dollars total."

"I've never heard of a physical being part of psychotherapy." Penny was feeling uneasy again.

"It is only proper and ethical," the doctor assured her. "Before proceeding with the therapy, I must determine if anything physical might be causing your emotional distress."

"Oh, I see," said Penny, almost apologetically.

"Now, Nurse Aphrodyte will show you to the examination room and prepare you. It won't take long, and if everything is in order, we'll proceed with the therapy."

As Penny disrobed in the examination room, she looked at herself in a full-length mirror built into the wall. Oddly enough, it was the first time in her life that she had seen herself completely nude. Not bad for thirty-eight, she thought, not bad at all. Pickthorn-Henriksen, standing on the other side of the two-way mirror, couldn't have agreed more. She's got the body of a teenager, he thought to himself as he headed for the examination room.

When he entered, Penny had just finished putting on the green hospital gown that Nurse Aphrodyte had given her. The doctor smiled at his patient and proceeded to conduct a very thorough and professional examination in record time. After Penny dressed, she rejoined him in his office.

"Well, Miss Penny, you seem the picture of physical health, except for a couple of minor things. You weighed one twenty-eight, not one twenty-six, so that will be one dollar more. And did you know that your blood pressure is slightly high?"

"No," she said, "it's normally a bit low."

"Well, then," Pickthorn-Henriksen said, grinning, "that will cost you five dollars more, for a total of sixty-nine for the examination."

"Five dollars more? For what?"

"For telling you something that you didn't know, Miss Penny. Now, do you have any questions before we begin the therapy?"

"Well, Doctor, I brought the manuscript of my novel. I thought that if you looked it over, it might help you analyze my problem. A lot of my experiences and fantasies are right here," she said, thumping the manuscript as she handed it to him.

"I see," said Pickthorn-Henriksen, clearing his throat. "That's really the type of thing that we should explore on the couch . . . in therapy. Now Nurse Aphrodyte will show you to the therapy room. Lie down and relax there for a while, and I'll join you shortly." He rippled the pages of the thick manuscript, looked at Penny, and smiled.

"Nurse Aphrodyte," he yelled toward his open office door. She appeared in an instant. "Nurse Aphrodyte, please show Miss Penny to therapy room C. Thank you."

Nurse Aphrodyte took Penny by the hand, led her into the room, reminded her to relax, and left, whispering to herself as she closed the door behind her.

Penny stood there for a moment, feeling a little like Alice in Wonderland in the huge, almost empty room. The walls were paneled with oak and the floor covered with a plush, bright red carpet. There were no windows at all, and the furniture consisted of a single chair and a king-size water couch or, more appropriately, water divan, in the middle of the floor. Penny kicked off her shoes, lay down in the giant divan, and began to feel very small indeed. Her gaze was drawn to the wall in front of her, though she didn't know why. She was unaware that subliminal messages were being flashed on the wall—soothing sights interspersed with pornographic pictures. Time began to drift away.

When Pickthorn-Henriksen entered the room and asked in a soothing voice if she was ready to begin, Penny was in something of a trance.

"Oh, yes, Doctor," she whispered. "Shall I start with chapter one?"

"Yes, I think that would be appropriate," he whispered back.

As Penny began, Pickthorn-Henriksen manipulated several buttons installed in the floor directly beneath his chair. Within a minute, the lights had dimmed and the oak paneling began moving down, almost imperceptibly. By the time Penny finished chapter two, an hour had passed. The paneling had disappeared into the floors, and except for the wall in front of Penny, they were surrounded by floor-to-ceiling mirrors with low-level colored light flashing through the room.

A detailed account of what happened over the next several hours need not be related here. Suffice it to say that by the time the session was over, Pickthorn-Henriksen had helped Penny demonstrate every chapter of her book before limping away with his clothes tucked under his arm.

Pickthorn-Henriksen thought he knew it all, thought he had at least seen it all. But after leaving the therapy room, he sat in his office for two hours making notes for sessions with future patients. "Straight A student in sexual awareness," he mumbled to himself. "Hell, she should be teaching a master's program." What they didn't do on the divan was accomplished on the floor or up against the wall. The good doctor decided to save the videotape for staff training.

Two days later, LaMarr Horsendork delivered the audio tapes, made from the bug, to Buck. After LaMarr left, Buck locked his door, mounted his Texas Ranger saddle, and sat glassy-eyed for several hours, listening to the tapes.

When Penny arrived at Cuddle Cove, Wanda took one look at her and knew that something terrible had happened. "What the hell happened to you?" she wanted to know. "You look like you just got through running the Boston Marathon."

"I feel worse than that," Penny cried. "I feel just terrible."

"There, there, Penny dear," she murmured. "Tell Wanda all about it. Get it off your chest." And so, for the next hour, choking back tears, Penny did. "Oh, my God," Wanda cried. "Did that terrible brute hurt you?"

"Oh, Wanda, it's worse than that."

"Worse! What could possibly be worse than *male* physical abuse!" Wanda was furious.

"I LOVED IT!" Penny screamed. "I LOVED IT! I LOVED IT! I LOVED IT!" She sat sobbing. "Oh, Wanda, what am I going to do? I could have stayed in a cottage—for more intensive therapy. I wanted to stay. I hated to leave."

"Penny, Penny," Wanda said, now under control. "Calm down. It's not too late. We'll find someone to help you. I promise."

Three days later, after dozens of phone calls, Wanda located a gay psychiatrist, Dr. Horace Katt, in San Francisco. Dr. Katt had never treated a woman before, but he reluctantly deferred to the chief justice and agreed to see Penny at least once. An appointment was made for the day after her interview with Sheriff Mullins.

Just what the doctor ordered, Wanda thought to herself as she hung up the phone, confident that Penny would be returning to the womb.

CHAPTER 11

As HIS PLANE FLEW downwind, turning into its base-leg flight
pattern over Mobile, Stoney Gilson looked out his window
and thought how cool and inviting the lush, green landscape
appeared. But when he walked out of the terminal with his one
small bag, he felt consumed by the tepid, humid air, his body
and clothing suddenly damp. As he walked across the pavement
to his rented car a short distance away, he could feel the steam
rising up under his pantlegs from cement that had been covered
with a torrent of warm rainwater just two hours earlier.

Driving toward Mobile, he knew where he wanted to go but,
without a map, not how to get there. He soon found himself by
the docks on the west side of the bay. He could see the old
causeway and the interstate crossing to the other side, but he
decided to ask for more precise directions both for getting across
the bay and, more importantly, for getting to Missie Jefferson's
house in Lake Forest. He stopped his car where several large
tugboats were tied up to the dock. In front of the dock sat a small
house trailer with a sign above the door that said: Rebel Tug

Service, Inc. Below that, another sign stated simply: Office.

Stoney left his car and walked the short distance to the office. As he let himself in, he almost bumped into an old cluttered desk that nearly blocked the door. Behind it sat a middle-aged man with black, graying hair. He was wearing blue jeans, a navy blue polo shirt, and a navy blue yachting cap—the crown crushed with crossed gold anchors embroidered on the front.

"How do you do, sir," Stoney said warmly. "My name is Stoney Gilson. Are you the manager here?"

"I ain't the goddamn deckhand," the man answered crustily, "and I ain't no damn manager neither. Ain't no such thing as a manager of a tugboat. I'm the cap'n of this outfit, and you sound like a goddamn Yankee."

"Well, not really, Captain. I'm from California." He grinned, enjoying the Cap'n.

"Same goddamn thing!" said the captain, extending his right hand to Stoney and snuffing out a Camel cigarette with the other. The smile that broke out on his face exposed teeth that were brown with tobacco stains. "Cap'n Manders is my name—Alexander Manders—but I guess you can call me Cap'n even if you are a goddamn Yankee. What can I do for ya?"

Stoney shook hands and said, "I need some directions, Cap'n." He handed over a note with Missie Jefferson's name and address printed on it.

"Hell, that's my old house!" roared the captain. "Sold it to her two years ago. Nice old lady. Neighbors think she's the maid, caretaker. They're still wonderin' when the heck the owners are gonna show up. Ha!" he laughed.

"Yeah," he continued. "I'm livin' on the boats now. Kids are all grown an' gone. The wife ran off with some uppity bastard named Lenny. Kindly relieved me of my goddamned bank account before she left."

"I'm real sorry to hear that."

"Sorry!" the captain roared again. "Hell, son, I've never been happier in my life. Now let me draw you a map. I'd tell you how to get there, but bein' a damn Yankee, you'd forget ever'thin' I said before you got halfway across the interstate." He smiled his brown-toothed smile again.

Fifteen minutes later, Stoney pulled his car to a stop in front of Missie's home in Lake Forest. The large, two-story brick house had white columns in the front and was surrounded by tall pine trees. He could see a small black face peeking at him from behind a curtain in a second-story window. He walked to the front door and rapped the brass knocker a couple of times against the solid wood. The door slowly opened about halfway.

"Missie Jefferson?"

"Yes," she said cautiously, looking Stoney up and down. "How do you know me?"

"I'm Stoney Gilson, Missie, from Sacramento, D.C. I'm a reporter for the *Sacramento Bunion*. We met when I did a story on Senator Baal a few years ago."

"Oh, yeah, I 'member now," she said, grinning. "How you been? Come on in." She closed the door behind him and led him up a short flight of stairs to a modestly furnished living room. "Have a seat," she said, pointing him to the nicest chair. "What brings you all the way out here—to my house?"

Instead of answering her question, Stoney said, "This sure is a lovely home you have here, Missie. You seem to be enjoying a comfortable retirement. I think you're very fortunate."

"Well, yeah, I guess that's so. I worked over fo'ty years for the senator and Miss Daphne, and now they're doin' right by me. Can't complain 'bout that."

As Stoney and Missie continued to make small talk, the generous retirement benefits kept flickering in his mind, kindling various thoughts, but he discounted anything dishonest. The Baals could well afford to take care of fifty Missies, and besides, Missie did not appear to be the dishonest type.

After another half hour of superficial chatter, Stoney decided that the atmosphere was as warm as it was going to get, so he explained to Missie the reason for his visit—he wanted to hear anything and everything that she knew about J.J. Would she mind answering a *few* questions?

"Mr. Stoney," she declared, "don't ask me nothin' 'bout Mr. J.J. If that's what you come all the way out here for, you can just turn aroun' and go right back."

"But, Missie, J.J. is a public figure. A governor—and maybe someday the president. The people have a right to know more about him."

"I know all 'bout public figures, Mr. Stoney, and I seen how Mr. J.J.'s been buildin' that wall and everything. Can't even go to visit out there anymore without one of them fancy credit cards."

Stoney stared at her for a moment before he understood that last statement. "No, no, Missie," he said, "it's not a credit card. A visa is a government paper that you get and it lets you visit somewhere for a while."

"Whatever it is," she said, her temper rising, "I think it's a bunch of pig shit—I mean hogwash," she corrected.

Stoney smiled. "So, will you talk with me, Missie? Just answer a few questions? Please."

"I done told you once, don't ask me nothin' 'bout that boy. What goes on in a man's house is private and no business of yours or anybody else "

"But, Missie, J.J. chose to become a public person. No one forced him into it. What if he gets to be president someday, sitting there in the White House with his finger on the button that could kill us all, and we don't even know who in God's name this man really is?" Stoney begged.

Missie sat silent for a moment, looking at the floor. Then, looking up, said, "I'm sorry, Mr. Stoney, I really am. I just can't tell you nothin'."

Disheartened but not yet defeated, Stoney tried another tack. "What about his friends? Can I ask about them?"

"That's fine, Mr. Stoney. Just don't ask me nothin' 'bout Georgie Mandrocci, 'cause I ain't sayin' nothin' 'bout him neither."

"Georgie Mandrocci, the congressman? He was a good friend of J.J.?"

"Yes, he was, at one time," Missie answered, "but I ain't got nothin' to say 'bout him."

"That's quite all right, Missie," Stoney assured her, unable to conceal a smile. "But thank you all the same. I won't have any more questions. You've been very kind to allow me into your home."

Missie, all smiles now that the interrogation was over, offered Stoney a late lunch, which he accepted. Stoney, who always enjoyed the company of truly sincere people, felt somewhat guilty about conning Missie out of the information she unknowingly gave him, and he reverted to small talk during lunch. Ninety minutes later, he was back at the Mobile Airport, bound for Washington, D.C.

Stoney didn't really expect to get any straight answers from Congressman Mandrocci. The most he hoped for was some indication that Buck's intuition was correct—something to pursue. Missie was strike one, Mandrocci would be strike two, and the whole thing was starting to cost him a lot of money.

When Stoney presented himself to Mandrocci's receptionist,

he was informed that the congressman was in a committee meeting and, further, that absolutely no one saw him without an appointment.

"When will he be back in his office?" Stoney asked the steely-eyed receptionist.

"In approximately two hours," came the reply through gritted teeth.

"Well, I'll be back then, Miss Trappe," Stoney said, getting her name off her nameplate. "Please tell the congressman that I have some personal questions concerning J.J. Baal. I think he'll want to see me." Stoney winked at the unreceptive receptionist. "See you in two hours."

To kill some time, Stoney took a cab to see the newly erected monuments to former presidents James Earl Carter, Jr., and Ronald Wilson Reagan. These eyesores, one constructed with Georgia cement and the other fashioned from California redwood, were concessions that Congress made to the Carter and Reagan families with the stipulation that if another Carter or Reagan were ever to run for public office anywhere at any time, they would be dynamited into piles of gravel and sawdust.

On the way back to the House Office Building, Stoney heard on the cab's radio that the United States had successfully launched a warhead into space and destroyed J.J.'s spy satellite. J.J. vowed that for every one shot down, he would launch two more in its place.

When Stoney walked through the door, Miss Trappe flashed a phony smile and led him into Georgie's spacious office. Georgie was seated at his handmade walnut desk, a ten-thousand-dollar token of appreciation from the Teamsters.

"Welcome, Mr. Gilson," said Georgie, rising to his feet. "Have a seat. Caroline, dear, please close the door on your way out. Thank you, dear." The two shook hands and then sat down, eyeing one another. "Now, Mr. Gilson, er . . . , Stoney. May I call you Stoney?"

"Certainly, Georgie," Stoney said, his smile growing as Georgie's faded.

"Well, then, Stoney, what can I do for you?"

"Well, as I think you know, I'm a reporter for the *Sacramento Bunion,* and I'm doing an in-depth feature on our governor. I understand that you and J.J. have been close friends for quite some time, and if you don't mind, I'd like to ask you a few personal questions."

"Well, Stoney," Georgie said, forcing a smile, "I really don't know how I can help you. My family and Daphne's people go back many, many years. Been friends a long time. J.J. and I went to private schools together, up through high school."

"Did you notice anything unusual about J.J. during your school years?" Stoney immediately regretted his question, knowing that any response would be less than truthful.

"Well, no," Georgie answered, looking very bored. "He was just one of the guys."

During the scant minute that he had been in Georgie's office, it became crystal clear to Stoney that he would get exactly what he expected—nothing. He needed to goad Georgie into some reaction. "Georgie," Stoney hesitated, "do you think that J.J might be a little bit . . ."—he raised his right hand to point near his right cheek, then let it fall limply forward, breaking at the wrist—"different?"

"What's that supposed to mean?" snarled Georgie.

He can't be that stupid, Stoney thought. "Might J.J. be just a teeny bit gay?"

The color started to drain from Georgie's face. "*What!*"

Without moving or changing his innocent expression, Stoney asked, "Is J.J. gay? You know, a queer, a fag, a fairy. Is J.J. a homo?"

"Get out of my office!" screamed the congressman.

"Were you two ever involved?" Stoney asked as he stood up.

"Get out of my fucking office!"

"I guess the interview's over," Stoney said as he backed up toward the door.

"Fuck you, you fucking fuckhead!"

Stoney caught a late plane back to Sacramento, D.C. The next morning, he phoned Buck on his private line.

"Hello," said the sheriff, trying to disguise his voice.

"It's all right, Buck. It's me, Stoney."

"Never know when somebody might misdial this number and recognize my voice," Buck said. "Then I'd have to have the damn number changed. What the hell do you want?"

"I've been to Alabama and to Washington, D.C., and now I'm sure you're right, but I can't prove it. I've got to work another angle. If I can put it together, I'll let you know."

"Is that it? That's all you got to say?"

"That's it, Buck."

"Goodbye."

"Goodbye, Buck."

Dumb little shit, Buck thought to himself, flies around the country to find out something I knew all along.

CHAPTER 12

AFTER STONEY LEFT his office, Georgie was so incensed that he fired Miss Trappe, carved Bobby Kennedy's name in the desk that he got from the Teamsters, and waited until dark to drive home so that he could stop and urinate on the James Earl Carter, Jr., monument. He tossed and turned in bed until he finally cried himself to sleep at three in the morning, hugging his Teddy Kennedy bear.

At 8:00 A.M. (5:00 A.M. PDT), he rolled J.J. out of bed with a phone call.

"Hello," J.J. mumbled, half asleep.

"J.J., this is Georgie. You awake?"

"In case you've forgotten, Georgie, it's five o'clock out here. What do you want?"

"He was here, J.J., that reporter from the *Bunion*. Gilson, Stoney Gilson. I don't know what he knows, but I'm sure he knows something."

"He what?"

"What I mean is," Georgie moaned, "I don't think he knows

anything specific. He thinks something is there but doesn't know where to find it. But why me? Why did he come to me!" Georgie cried.

"Oh, quit bawling, Georgie. You haven't got anything to worry about, not yet anyway."

"Nothin' to worry about!" Georgie nearly strangled his Teddy Kennedy bear. "J.J., the folks in Prichard are not very understanding about *that* sort of thing, even if it was a long time ago. I've got a wife and nine kids, J.J. What would they think? And what about my job, for fuck's sake?"

"Simmer down, Georgie. Nothing's going to happen," J.J. said reassuringly. "And what the hell, you've got enough money to last ten lifetimes." He laughed.

"It's no laughing matter, J.J.," Georgie admonished, "and it's not just the money. Hell, I'm living like a king. Ten cent shoeshines, free food, booze, sauna, unlimited *secretarial* help, just to mention a few things. My mistress and two kids in Arlington. Plus I'm trying out a new one over in Cheverly. A little black girl. Sure would hate to give her up so soon. She's an expert in bondage."

"Will you quit your goddamn bawling, Georgie. You're making me sick for Chrissakes."

"J.J.," Georgie whimpered, "you just don't understand the seriousness of this thing. I'm unemployable if I lose this job. I've been in Congress for ten years. I haven't even had to *think* since the day I entered the U. of A. Stump O'Leary tells me how to vote, and when he doesn't, the Teamsters do. I've got it made here. I don't even have to campaign. Every two years Toni runs around Prichard with her boobs flopping, yelling 'Vote for Georgie,' and they do.

"J.J., if they get ahold of this shit, they'll crucify me. Jesus Christ. Other guys screw up and come out smelling like perfume. Look at that goddamn Teddy. He'll die in that Senate seat like that girl who died in his back seat. Him and that fucking Hartpence . . . teaming up . . . franchising *Hartpence & Kennedy Homes for Unwed Mothers*. 'If you don't qualify, we will personally assist you until you do. We guarantee it or your money back!' Can you believe that shit . . . and they're making millions. But *me*, I'll be hung out to dry. Then what'll I do?"

"Look, Georgie," said J.J., finally allowed to speak again, "if Gilson had anything, he wouldn't have come to you. He was probably just trying to get a reaction out of you. You didn't give him one, did you?"

"Oh, heavens no. No way, J.J. I was so cool that that asshole probably thought he was talking to an Eskimo in a deep freeze. Ha ha," Georgie forced a crippled laugh.

"Just try to relax, Georgie. I'm the one he's after. He can't prove what happened between us, and if he can't prove it, he won't use it, not Gilson. That idiot sheriff, Buck Mullins, probably sent him on this little fishing expedition."

"Well, I hope you're right," Georgie moaned. "Folks in Prichard wouldn't care less that it happened almost twenty-five years ago or that you paid me. Shit! And I didn't even need the money. All this for a lousy five bucks." He threw his Teddy Kennedy bear against the wall, then walked over and stepped on its neck.

CHAPTER 13

DURING THE DAYS between her marathon session with Dr. Pickthorn-Henriksen and her interview with Buck, Penny took a vacation, sunbathing in the nude next to the pool in her back yard. Cuddle Cove received maximum protection from the sheriff's helicopter patrol during those few days, and by the end of the week, her picture was securely taped to the inside of every deputy's locker in the sheriff's patrol division. When she wasn't sunbathing, Penny was shopping for new clothes and having her hair cut and styled. She was well aware of what she was doing, and though she knew it was supposed to bother her, it didn't. Penny was blossoming. Wanda took it all in but didn't say anything. She was confident that Penny would return to normal after her visit with Dr. Horace Katt.

On the day of the interview with Buck, Penny wore a matching yellow skirt and blouse that accented her tan. The skirt was cut at the knee and the form-fitting blouse, although buttoned to the top, was nonetheless revealing. Her makeup was not heavy but adequate. She was easily one of the most stunning women ever to walk the halls of the Sacramento Sheriff's Department.

When she entered the lobby, the deputies at the public counter froze with instant recognition. But they didn't see the pretty Penny in the yellow outfit. They saw her laid out on a diving board, stark naked, and they couldn't believe their eyes—a photograph come to life.

"I don't believe it," said one officer to another.

"Believe what?"

"That she's a lesbo. Can't be."

"Well, she is. Shacked up with the homeliest dog you ever laid eyes on."

"What a fucking waste. It makes me sick."

After the formalities of gaining entrance and directions to Buck's office, which the officers stretched for as long as possible, Penny was on her way.

"I don't believe it. I won't believe it!" the first officer said as he broke into a run for the locker room to check the picture pasted in his locker, just to be sure.

"It's her. Sure the hell is, damn," he said, as he walked back to the lobby, sulkily.

After getting past a receptionist, Penny stood before Brenda. "I'm here to see Sheriff Mullins."

"I'm sorry," Brenda said sweetly, "but the sheriff is due to give an interview shortly. I'll have to schedule you for another time."

"Yes, I know," Penny said. "I'm the interviewer—Penny Penny from the *Bunion*."

"Oh, mercy," said Brenda, who had expected Penny to look like a hippie Raggedy Ann. "Follow me, please," she recovered. "The sheriff is expecting you."

Buck had seen the picture that all the deputies had, but when he saw Penny in the flesh, his heart dropped to his crotch, where it was right at home. He greeted her, motioned her to a chair in front of his desk, and then sat down quickly before she could notice that his enlarged "heart" was beginning to pulsate.

"Well, Sheriff, your office is certainly everything I was told it was. Do you mind if I take a look around before we begin?"

"Not at all, Miss Penny," Buck said proudly. He started to rise and join her but thought better of it.

"My, my, Sheriff, you certainly have been honored often enough. There must be a hundred plaques on that wall," Penny said sincerely.

"Oh, it's really not all that much, Miss Penny," Buck blushed. "For a man who's been in office for as long as I have, it's really not that much."

Penny moved to the far end of the office. "Oh, Sheriff, what a magnificent portrait!" she exclaimed. "When did you find time to be an army general?"

Buck was now standing behind her, studying her curves and taking in the heady mix of soap laced with perfume. Buck had a sudden, terrible urge to mount up. He cleared his throat, where there was also a lump. "That's not an army uniform, Miss Penny. That's my official sheriff's formal combat uniform. My family and friends commissioned that portrait several years ago as sort of a token of their appreciation." Buck saw no reason for the truth of the matter to go beyond himself and the folks at Wells Fargo MasterCard.

"Well, well, this certainly is some office," said Penny in admiration as she moved across the room to the wall of photographs. "My, my, look at all the famous people you know." She stopped in front of the picture of J. Edgar Hoover and studied it for a moment. "Oh dear," she said. "Did you get this one at a seance, Sheriff?" Penny started to laugh. "That old boy had been dead for two years when he signed it. See?" she said, pointing to the date written under the signature.

"Well," Buck stammered, clearing another lump from his throat, "come to think of it, he was a bit in his cups when he gave me that. Put down the wrong damn date. How do you like that? Why, Miss Penny, I never even noticed that before." Buck forced a laugh and thought to himself, your time's coming, bitch.

As she studied the photographs, Penny recognized that several had similar handwriting. She smiled inwardly as she walked to the chair and seated herself in front of Buck's desk. She placed her purse in front of her, on the desk.

Buck smiled as he sat down but then glared at the purse. "Well, that's the tour, Miss Penny. Now, what can I do for you?"

"Well, Sheriff, as I said on the phone, your name is being prominently mentioned as a possible gubernatorial candidate in next year's Democratic primary, and the *Bunion* wants to be the first paper to do a feature story on you. To give its readers a sneak preview, so to speak."

It's a *sneak* all right, you fucking cunt, Buck thought to himself, then smiled broadly. "And as I told you, Miss Penny, I've made no decisions along those lines. But I'll tell you one thing, if I do get involved, it will be a herculean effort." Then he added, looking at her empty hands, "By the way, did you forget your notebook? I can loan you a pencil and paper."

"Oh, no, Sheriff. Thanks, but I have them right here in my purse." Penny carefully removed a notebook and pencil from her purse and then returned it to the desk. "Let's see now," she mulled, "as I understand it, you grew up in a little town called Tater, in Oklahoma."

"That's right," said Buck, leaning back in his chair and looking nostalgic. "That's where I grew up. That's where I played my high school ball."

"Ball?"

"Football. I made All City four years in a row and All State the last two." As Buck lied in earnest, Sheriff Henry Lukins rolled over in his grave. Tater didn't have a high school, and the only balls that Buck ever saw in Tater were the cotton balls that he picked and threw into the big sack dragging along behind him.

"Then, after high school," he continued, "I was neck-deep in scholarship offers. Oklahoma wanted me real bad, and so did State, but I went with Texas. The people in Oklahoma didn't cotton to that."

"I'll bet," said Penny. "What position did you play, Sheriff?"

"Fullback. Yep, they used me like a goddamn battering ram. 'Scuse my language, Miss Penny." Buck smiled as he pictured what never happened as though it happened only yesterday. "But it all came to an end in summer practice before my first season with Texas."

"What happened?" asked Penny, concerned.

"Shattered my ankle in the first damn scrimmage," Buck grimaced. "They had every specialist in the country look at it. Even flew one in from Switzerland. But they all agreed that my ball-playing days were over." Buck seemed in great pain as he studied the wood grain of his desk. Then he seemed to gather himself. He looked up and smiled. "But I survived. The good Lord helps those who help themselves."

"What did you do, Sheriff? Did you stay on at the university?"

109

"No, I didn't, Miss Penny. I drifted around the oil rigs for a month or two, pretty disillusioned. That's when I became a cowboy. Herded cattle all over southwest Texas for three years," he said, "and over there's the old saddle I used. It belonged to a retired Texas Ranger who gave it to me when I first started out. Sure brings back memories." Just now, Buck was remembering when he bought the saddle at a garage sale in Bakersfield, California.

"Then how did you end up in law enforcement here in Sacramento, D.C.?" Penny asked.

"Well, Miss Penny, Sheriff Lukins was a good friend of the family." There was another rumbling under the headstone of Henry Lukins. "He had kin in Tater and was a big fan of mine. The old boy loved football. After I broke my ankle and lost out on a pro or even a college career, he begged me to come to work for him. Which I eventually did, obviously. And, Miss Penny, it all turned out for the best," he said with a sweep of his hand that took in his photographs, his plaques, and the authority of his present position.

"Well, you certainly have had an interesting life and illustrious career, Sheriff Mullins," remarked Penny with some real admiration. "And it looks like your son Buster is following right along in your footsteps."

"He certainly is," beamed Buck. "Buster is a captain now, and someday he'll be sheriff. I was the youngest man ever elected to this office, and when I raised my right hand to be sworn in, I told young Buster that he'd be the second youngest. And I think I'll be proven right, Miss Penny."

Their conversation continued amiably for another hour, with Penny asking harmless questions and Buck lying through his teeth. Sheriff Lukins never had so much exercise in such a short period

110

of time. Then, according to her plan, Penny began to ask increasingly substantial questions, warming Buck up for the big one. And Buck, according to *his* plan, became increasingly caustic and slipped slowly, intentionally, into his profane, slang-filled vocabulary, warming up for *his* grand finale. Buck knew what Penny was up to, but she had no idea what he was up to, and that was his advantage. She expected him to become more and more defensive and to gloss over his answers to her pointed questions. She was slightly shocked but clearly elated when his mouth turned into an overused but never cleaned Dempsey dumpster. Her notebook was filling up with spicy quotes.

When Buck concluded an expletive-saturated oration on J.J.'s Reverse Crime Control Master Plan, Penny asked, "Sheriff Mullins, though you have never been quoted for publication, it is rumored that you have made some pretty acrimonious remarks about our governor and his private life."

"Yeah, yeah," Buck acknowledged. "I've said a few things. I don't know that I'm ready to go public yet, but I'll tell you one thing—that little som'bitch is a herculean cocksucker if ever I saw one!"

"A *what?*"

"Cocksucker, dear. A queer, a goddamn faggot." Buck smiled, leaned back in his chair, and glanced at Penny's purse.

Penny was confused. She had expected negative replies but nothing like this. He's either up to something, doesn't give a damn, or is stark raving mad, she thought to herself. Probably all three. "Well, Sheriff," she said, raising her eyebrows, "you do get to the point."

"That's the best way, Miss Penny," he laughed. "Call 'em like you see 'em."

Penny stared at him intently. "Speaking of the gay lifestyle, Sheriff, how do you view our beautiful city by the Bay and its gay community?"

"Miss Penny," Buck scowled, "if you're referring to that god-damn pack of queers in San Francisco, that's got to be the sorriest pile of dogshit ever assembled in one spot on this earth."

"Why, Sheriff, you seem to be defaming a world-renowned city—one of the most beautiful, delightful. . ."

"Don't give me that shit, Miss Penny!" Buck was on a bit of a roll. "When I came out here, the place was thirty percent queer, and before you knew it, it was fifty percent. Now it must be about ninety-nine goddamn percent. Hell, the mayor, the chief of police, even their fucking sheriff—they're all flaming faggots! Find me a som'bitch in that hellhole who isn't a faggot! A bunch of heath-enistic, feet stinkin', Jesus hatin' som'bitches." Buck was on his feet now, raving, pacing around Penny, glaring. She sat in wide-eyed wonder, looking up at him, glued to her chair. This was getting good. "San Francisco, shit!" screamed Buck Mullins. "It's nothin' but a rock crawlin' with cocksuckers and dildo-wavin' bull-dikes. It's just another Sodom—Sodom-by-the-Sea. That rock is goin' to roll right into the ocean some day. You can mark my words on that, Miss Reporter. Then we'll see if faggots float." Quite satisfied with his performance, the sheriff took a deep breath and sat down.

"Do you consider yourself something of a prophet, Sheriff?"

"A what?"

"A prophet. You said that San Francisco was going to roll into the ocean. Is that some sort of prophecy? Has the Big Guy been whispering in your ear? Have you been talking to God, Sheriff?"

"Call it whatever you want," sneered Buck. "But that dung hill is sure as hell going to fall off into the ocean. So you'd better tell that bunch of heathens to start practicin' how to breathe under water."

"Thank you so very much, Sheriff," said Penny with a wide smile. She folded up her notebook and inserted her pencil in the spiral rings. Still smiling, she continued, "Without a doubt, Sheriff, you are the crudest, most barbaric, and most preposterous fraud that I have ever had the *pleasure* of talking to. Those pictures on your wall. What a laugh. I bet that half of them are forgeries. 'Hoover was in his cups.' Ha! Hoover signed his name with a very distinctive *J*, and that most certainly isn't it. And it looks to me like someone at a plaque company owed you a lot of favors, Sheriff. Thank you kindly for the interview. I'm quite sure that I have all that I need." Penny was laughing hysterically as she got up to leave. "Don't bother getting up, Sheriff," she chuckled. "I'll show myself out."

"You simple *cunt!*" Buck was on his feet in an instant.

Penny stopped and turned around. She wasn't laughing anymore. "What did you call me, Sheriff?"

"A cunt, Miss Penny. You're a cunt. There are girls, ladies, women, and cunts. You're a cunt. You think I didn't know that you were coming here to do a number on me?"

"I just know that I got exactly what I came after, Mister Hotshot Sheriff!"

"You got your half, cunt, now I'm gettin' mine," spat Buck through gritted teeth. "And you're gonna remember, when it comes to nut-cuttin' time, you don't screw with old Buck Mullins, you goofy bitch."

As Penny turned again toward the door, Buck grabbed her

113

purse, wrenched it open, and dumped its contents on his desk. The miniature recorder clattered out, top first, the tape still turning.

"Ahhh!" Penny screamed. "Are you crazy? Give me that!" she yelled, reaching for the recorder.

"About *twice* as crazy as you had me figured for, you stupid cunt." Buck snatched up the recorder, yanked out the tape, and stuck the cassette in his pocket. Then he threw the recorder on the floor and crushed it with the heel of his boot.

"Now I want you to hear something, little lady," said the sheriff with a demonic grin. He pulled a tape recorder of his own from a desk drawer and pushed the play button. As the tape began to roll, Penny began to sway on shaky legs. Moans, groans, giggles, and heavy breathing blared from the speaker, followed by the hideous giggle of Dr. Hubert Pickthorn-Henriksen.

"You rotten bastard!" screamed Penny, now shaking uncontrollably. "*You dirty rotten bastard!*"

"Get out of here, you dumb cunt, and don't forget what I said, when it comes to nut-cuttin' time you don't fuck with old Buck!"

Penny started sweeping her things from Buck's desk back into her purse.

"Don't forget this," Buck said, reaching into his drawer and tossing Little Wanda out on the desktop.

"OH! Oh, oh, oh," Penny cried. "Oh, no!" She grabbed Little Wanda, stuffed it into her purse, and stumbled to the door. "You animal. YOU ROTTEN ANIMAL!" she screamed.

"And when you write your story," called Buck, "don't forget what I've got, including blowups of that ramrod you call Wanda." Buck cackled, his arms folded across his chest, thinking about how much fun this had been.

"Screw you, Mr. Sheriff," Penny cried. "I don't give a damn what you've got. I'm going to blister your fat ass!"

"Well, don't forget, Miss Penny Penny," Buck said calmly, "when you get in a pissin' contest, it flows both ways."

Penny slammed the door so hard that Buck's portrait tilted slightly to the right and two plaques tumbled from the wall. Buck stood there for a moment, grinning, until he became aware of the erotic sounds still blaring from the tape recorder. He took a few deep breaths, walked over to his Texas Ranger saddle, and mounted up.

CHAPTER 14

PENNY WENT DIRECTLY to the *Bunion*. After regaining her composure in the women's lounge, Penny made a few phone calls to Oklahoma and Texas to verify some "facts," and then went to work on her story. Four hours later, as promised, she had written a story designed to blister the sheriff's fat ass. She handed the finished product to Axel Rodd.

"Here's *your* story, Axel," Penny said firmly. "I hope it's a good one because it's my last. I'm through. Through with this business. Through with Sacramento, D.C., and everything in it. Goodbye!" And with that, she stormed out the door.

Axel stormed right after her. "Get your ass back in here, Penny! Get your goddamned *ass* back in this office. NOW!" But neither Axel Rodd nor anyone else at the *Bunion* ever saw Penny again.

Penny drove straight to Cuddle Cove, where she packed three new outfits, showered and put on some fresh clothes, and left Wanda a note advising that she'd be back in a couple of days. Then she drove down Highway 80 and crossed the bridge to the city by the bay. She checked into the Hotel Gomorrah, south of Market, and got a good night's sleep.

Penny awoke at about nine, showered and dressed, and walked out into the fresh, crisp morning air. It was so nice that she decided to walk to the office of Dr. Horace Katt. Penny loved the openness of the city—the problem of heterosexuality almost eliminated. She smiled as she passed a policeman kissing a garbage collector. It was one of those days in San Francisco.

She stepped into a coffeeshop for a cup of hot tea and read the morning paper. The city was abuzz with the news of the quickie marriage of Chief of Police Walter Fowler and his secretary, John Flannigan. They had been married in a small civil ceremony the day before, with Mayor Joe Damien serving as the maid of honor, and had left for a honeymoon at an undisclosed location in Greece.

Penny had spent a lot of time in San Francisco during her college days and had always enjoyed being there, but strange emotions were churning inside of her, and just now she felt a little out of step, a little out of place. She had intended to see the Coit Tower. With its recently installed fountain and pink carnations planted at the top, Penny thought that the tower must look almost identical to Little Wanda. But just now she didn't really have the desire to see it. It's not going anywhere, she thought to herself. Another time.

Penny was carrying her manuscript under one arm and Little Wanda in her purse. When she passed a Salvation Army Collection Box, she paused, the urge to deposit Little Wanda very strong. Some deserving soul could surely use her, Penny thought to herself. But when she continued on, Little Wanda remained in her purse. Although troubled, Penny felt good and was looking forward to her visit with Dr. Katt.

The doctor's office was located in a remodeled Victorian. The reception area was comfortable and tastefully furnished, with a small fireplace in the far wall. Maggie Irish, the petite, attractive receptionist-secretary who greeted her, wore the traditional engagement and wedding rings on her left hand and had pictures of her young children on her desk. She lived in Oakland and came to work for Dr. Katt after her husband found her the job, knowing that it was a safe place for his amorous young wife to work. Dr. Katt, a progressive, hired Maggie long before it became necessary for the city to pass an ordinance banning discrimination in the hiring of heterosexuals.

Dr. Horace Katt—tall, dark, and handsome—was thirty-six, slender, and looked a bit like Stoney Gilson, with close-cropped hair, glasses, and a natural, sincere smile that needed no prompting.

Katt originally enrolled at the University of California at Davis Veterinary School, but he switched to people when he discovered that he was allergic to cats. After becoming a psychiatrist, he specialized in the treatment of emotionally disturbed males with heterosexual tendencies. Horace, a thorough professional, didn't dislike women—he liked everyone and everything—he just never saw the need for them and so never went out of his way to have anything to do with one. Penny would be his first real contact with a female, and he looked forward to it with professional enthusiasm.

Maggie, who had conjured an image in her mind of a plain, dull, used-up Penny, nearly went into shock when the strikingly beautiful woman walked through the door. Dr. Katt, similarly affected, quickly sat down before his legs turned to Jell-O. Penny took one look at him and thought that she must be in the wrong office until she noticed the framed pinups of Oscar Wilde, Gore Vidal, and Jerry Brown hanging on the office walls.

119

Penny felt a stirring in her loins, and a satisfied smile spread across her face. Horace was dumbfounded. His computer mind started running wild, with no reference to lock on to. His intellect told him he was dealing with a totally new, mysterious emotion that required exploration, professional exploration.

Maggie, thinking that there must be some mistake, asked, "Yes, miss, can we help you?"

"Yes! I'm Penny Penny. I'm here to see Doctor Katt," she said, still smiling, holding out her hand to Horace. "You are Doctor Katt, I hope, er, I . . . I assume."

"Yes. Yes, I am," answered the doctor, recovering his balance and composure. He took Penny's hand and gave it a light, professional shake. "This is Mrs. Irish," he added, nodding to Maggie.

"Maggie," said Maggie, giggling with recognition of what she thought could never occur in that office. "Pleased to meet you!"

"My pleasure, Maggie," Penny responded, shaking her hand too.

After briefly discussing her concerns, Horace assured Penny that he was an expert in the problem of heterosexual tendencies and was confident that he could help her, even though he had never treated a female patient before. And, yes, he would peruse her manuscript while she filled out the necessary forms. "Now, if you have no further questions," he smiled, "we'll begin the session right after you fill out the forms for our files."

"Will you be doing a physical examination first, Doctor?" Penny said, looking longingly at Horace.

Horace blushed. "Well, I don't normally do that sort of thing myself. If something physical appears to be involved, I'll refer you to another doctor for that." He smiled again.

"Oh, okay," Penny said, disappointed.

Unlike Dr. Pickthorn-Henriksen, Horace took a professional

interest in Penny's manuscript and scanned it intently while Penny filled out the forms in the other room. The mysterious feeling churning inside of him intensified, but he was still unable to identify its source. His computer mind was racing through its files but finding nothing that could help.

The therapy session proceeded routinely until they got into the contents of the manuscript. Horace became a bit nervous, while Penny, responding without the prompting afforded her by Dr. Pickthorn-Henriksen, asked Horace to close the drapes and dim the lights at the end of chapter one. At the end of chapter two, she stood up between Horace and the couch, pointed to the single bow tie that held her wraparound dress together, and said, "Pull."

"P-p, pu, pu-pull," Horace stammered, wide-eyed.

"Pull, Doctor!" Penny ordered.

Horace, his hand shaking violently, managed to grasp one end of the tie, but when he hesitated, Penny spun around in place. The dress peeled off her body and fell to the floor. Horace sat stunned, still clutching the tie end and staring at her naked, glistening, suntanned body.

"AAHHHhhh!" he yelled as circuits shorted and chips crumbled in his computer. Animal instinct and pioneering spirit took over, driving him to attack and conquer the unknown.

As with other episodes of this nature, the details of what occurred will not be related here. Suffice to say that what took Pickthorn-Henriksen six and one-half hours to accomplish, Horace mastered in four. Penny, a veritable guru, had found an adoring disciple. It was her crowning glory.

Horace sent Maggie out for champagne and, when she returned, gave her a fat check as severance pay and told her that he would be giving up his practice in San Francisco.

Horace started a fire in the formerly unused fireplace, and as they toasted new love, he burned his pinups one at a time. And as Jerry Brown curled up in flames, Penny threw in Little Wanda.

Late that night, Penny called Wanda. After some small talk and a detailed discussion of what happened in the sheriff's office the previous day, Penny got to the point. "Wanda, I . . . I'm in Las Vegas."

"Oh, Penny, for crying out loud. What on earth ever possessed you? You don't even gamble."

"I got married, Wanda." Penny's short sentence was delivered like a staccato burst of machine gun fire.

"You what?" Then it registered. "YOU WHAT?" Wanda screamed. "Oh, Penny. No, no, no. Tell me it isn't true. Oh, Penny, how could you? Goddamnit! Who is she? Do I know her?"

"It's not a her. It's Doctor Katt. I'm Mrs. Horace Katt."

"Oh, no . . . no!" Wanda screamed again. "Oh, God, no. Oh, Penny, how? That . . . that just can't *possibly* be," she sobbed.

"Oh, Wanda, don't cry," Penny pleaded. "I'll explain everything when you're feeling better."

"Oh, oh, oh, oh," Wanda moaned.

"We're going to live in San Diego," Penny continued. "His parents live there. He's going to open an office there, changing his specialization to gynecology. I know everything will work out for the best."

"Are you really married-married?" Wanda moaned.

"Yes, we're really married-married, Wanda," Penny said. "And when we get to San Diego we'll get remarried in a Catholic church."

"You . . . in a Catholic church?" Wanda said, surprised.

"Oh, it's no problem," said Penny. "Neither of us has been married before, so all we have to do is confess."

"That'll take *you* a month," Wanda said sarcastically, hostility beginning to replace her tears.

"Oh, Wanda, don't get too angry," Penny pleaded. "I'll call you tomorrow, when you're feeling better. We'll figure something out. We always have."

"Okay, Penny," Wanda said skeptically. "Good night."

"Good night, Wanda," Penny said, sadly.

That night Wanda went to bed feeling all alone in the world, and she cried. But late the next morning she had another long conversation with Penny and a decision was reached.

After finishing her conversation with Penny, Wanda quickly dialed another number. "Yes, ma'am," she said to the female voice answering her call. "I need to make an appointment with Dr. Pickthorn-Henriksen. As soon as possible!"

CHAPTER 15

O N THE DAY following Penny's marriage, Axel unloaded on
Buck with both barrels. The first edition of the *Bunion*
carried a double banner headline: SHERIFF TALKS TO GOD!
and ONE MILLION $ SUNK IN CROTCH. The minute the
paper hit the streets, KROK-AM, KROK-FM, and KROK-TV
began broadcasting the stories every hour on the hour. By noon
every radio and television station in the area was putting Buck
through the shredder.

Penny had left nothing out of her story (except what he said
about J.J.), quoting him without mercy, profanities and all. The
lead paragraphs related his Sodom-by-the-Sea pronouncements
and ended with his "fantasy world of a football hero."

"No one associated with athletics in Texas or Oklahoma could
recall or verify with records the all-star football player Buck Mullins," she wrote. "However, it was confirmed that our sheriff did
receive one high honor. The town clerk of Tater, Oklahoma,
verified that at age sixteen, Sheriff Mullins, then known as Chet,
won the Tater All-Star Cotton Picking Championship. He went

125

on to compete at the state level, where he was eliminated in the first round by a twelve-year-old girl from Oklahoma City."

Harmony Nerd hammered away at the cost of the Crotch investigation and the paucity of results. "While our fine sheriff lounges in his tax-supported palace, Crotch continues to hold the community in terror," she wrote. A sidebar carried her interview with the inconsolable owner of the canary that was turned into a diplegic invalid when Crotch pulled out its wing feathers, causing an uproar from the Sacramento, D.C., Canary Owners Association. By early afternoon they had pickets surrounding the sheriff's administration building.

A television reporter interviewed Bubu Becker, the manager of a large chain of grocery stores. "Sir," asked the reporter, "what impact has the Crotch case had on our economy, as you see it?"

"Well," said Bubu, smiling for the camera, "we have suffered a drastic decline in the sale of Dr. Pepper and pantyhose, but . . ."

"Thank you, sir, for your expert opinion." The reporter turned to the camera, shaking his head. "And there you have the sad story, ladies and gentlemen, of the economy crumbling at our feet. And why? Because, *it is alleged*, of an inept and bungled investigation into the terroristic activities of the infamous Crotch. This has been Thurman Raggtale, Jr., with another live, Action News, Eyewitness Account, brought to you by the station where the *news* always comes first."

Buck seethed until about three o'clock. Then he fired six rounds into his television and ordered Buster and his SWAT team to go up on the roof and drop tear gas on the pickets. With that accomplished, he telephoned Bubu Becker.

"Bubu, you're a back-stabbin' som'bitch, and I'll have your fat ass in a sling!"

126

"But Buck," Bubu pleaded.

"But Buck, bullshit! Just when I need my so-called friends, you join up with that bunch'a cutthroat cocksuckers!"

"Now wait a cotton-pickin' minute, Buck! I didn't say nothin'. That damn reporter cut me off. Hell, we're makin' out like bandits. Everybody's stockin' up with Royal Crown, and we got in a special supply of crotchless pantyhose. They cost us less and we charge more."

"Well, you should never've talked to the som'bitches in the first place!"

"Aw, come on, Buck," Bubu moaned, "you started this whole thing by shootin' off your mouth to that broad from the *Bunion*. Fullback for Texas, gimme a break!"

"Oh, fuck you, Bubu!" Buck slammed down the phone.

Buck fumbled with the tapes and the pictures of Little Wanda while contemplating his next move. He decided to call LaMarr before ripping the guts out of Axel Rodd.

"LaMarr, this is Buck," he said calmly. "What else have you got for me?"

"What else? You got it all, Buck." LaMarr laughed good-naturedly.

"I've got it all! You fuckin' pervert. I didn't pay you thousands of dollars for a pile of tape. What about the flat ass little faggot? Did you get anything on him, or did you forget about *that* half of the bargain?"

"Listen, Buck," LaMarr pleaded, "I did what I could. I burgled her house and that doctor's office, got the dildo and the tapes, and followed the gay one to L.A. four times. There's no way to stick with him, Buck. He's always got a driver, and he jumps out in the middle of traffic or who knows where and disappears."

127

"You worthless little shit, LaMarr! I oughta throw your ass in jail for flashin' our elevator operator."

"Hey, Buck," LaMarr said sincerely, "I've got an idea."

"Make it good, LaMarr."

"Why don't you ask God about it?" LaMarr laughed.

"Go fuck yourself, LaMarr!" Buck threw the phone against the wall, and half a dozen plaques fell in a heap. "Shit! Shit! SHIT! I ain't got a thing on that little faggot yet! But I'm gonna get me a hunk of a few of 'em." Buck picked up the phone. It was cracked, but, amazingly, it still worked. He dialed Axel's number.

"Good afternoon, ol' buddy," Axel said.

"Axel, you're a no-good rotten som'bitch!"

"Well, Buck, to quote an old philosopher, 'When you get in a pissin' contest, it flows both ways.' " Axel laughed uproariously.

"Well the piss is still flowin', you rotten cocksucker, and now it's my turn!" Buck said, gritting his teeth.

"Oh! Tell me all about it, you worthless tub of shit. Got a message from God?" Axel roared.

"I've got some shit here that I'm gonna ram right up that Penny Penny's ass, your ass, and the goddamned *Bunion*'s ass!"

Axel laughed. "I know what you've got, Buck, so let me tell you a few things. First of all, that dipshit isn't here anymore. She quit. Second, I don't give a damn, and third, if you try it, you're going to wind up in your own hoosegow."

"Is that right, Mister Newspaper Man. Well, let me tell you somethin'. Far as I know, I'm still the law around here, and ain't nobody gonna put the law in jail."

"You may be the law in this county, Buck, but you're nothing but a low-class, low-rent burglar. The Feds snack on thugs like you who violate people's civil rights. Hell, the FBI spends ninety percent of their fuckin' time throwing assholes like you in jail. Your own goddamn jail!"

Buck was silent for a moment. Then he said, "You just try it, wise guy, and I'll take that pervert chief justice with me."

"That's the whole point, you dumb bastard," Axel said. "But for right now, I've got your nuts hangin' on the end of a pitchfork, and I'm going to keep 'em there." He laughed, belched, passed some gas, and hung up.

"Axel! Axel, get back on this goddamned line! Axel! Well, fuck you, you som'bitch!" Buck threw the phone at J. Edgar Hoover but hit Dolly Parton, and shards of broken glass pierced Dolly's breast. "Oh, shit," moaned Buck. "What have I done?" Just then, his private phone rang.

"Hello." Buck didn't even try to disguise his voice.

"Hi, Buck. This is Stoney. Bad day, huh?"

"That ain't the half of it, you rotten som'bitch."

"Me? What are you talking about?"

"It's all your fault, goddamnit! You should've warned me about that fuckin' cunt. Now I'm in deep shit."

"But, Buck, I did warn you. You shouldn't have talked to her, and you certainly shouldn't have served up all those dynamite quotes. You're a reporter's dream."

"Well, goddamnit, Stoney, what the hell am I gonna do? You got anything new on that flat ass little faggot? I gotta have somethin'. I need help bad."

"Nothing yet, Buck," Stoney sympathized. "But I'm working on a deal. If anything comes of it, I'll let you know."

"Well, that leaves me one card left to play," Buck moaned.

"Not Redneck and Watermelon?"

"Yeah, it's a som'bitch, Stoney, but if they catch Crotch, I'll be in tall cott'n."

"And if they don't?"

"That's the chance you take with those crazy bastards. If anybody can do it, they can. They may not do it right, but then who's gonna know the difference?"

"Only them and Crotch, I guess."

"That's right, that's right." Buck smiled for the first time all day. "Stoney, I still think you're a good ol' boy." He laughed.

"Thanks, Buck. Talk to you later."

"Okay, Stoney." Buck walked over and picked up his regular phone from the pile of glass on the floor. It seemed indestructible. He called Ernie Ratfern, captain of detectives.

"Captain Ratfern."

"Ernie, this is the Sher'ff. What are *they* doin'?"

"Well, Redneck is working in robbery and Watermelon is in homicide. What's up?"

"What's up! You jackass. I'm trying to shovel neck-deep shit with a pitchfork, and you ask 'what's up.' "

"Sorry, Sheriff," Ernie said. You dumb shit, he thought to himself. Fat mouth.

"Put 'em on Crotch."

"Are you sure that's what you want, Sheriff?"

"What the fuck did I just say?!"

"Right, Sheriff," Ernie said politely while giving the phone the finger. "Do you want them to report to you for instructions?"

"Hell no, moron! I don't want those crazy bastards anywhere near my office. Just sic 'em on Crotch. Give them whatever they need—an old car, guns, knives, bombs, and whatever else those two maniacs use to catch bad guys."

"Will do, Sheriff." Ernie hung up the phone and walked out of his office whistling and smiling, looking for Redneck and Watermelon.

The day was nearing an end, and for the first time, Buck felt relaxed. He called Brenda on the intercom and told her to hold his calls. "I've got some *tall* thinkin' to do, honey."

He left his desk and walked over to the Texas Ranger saddle. He stood there for a moment, took three deep breaths, and mounted up.

He was charging across the flat Texas landscape, his horse covered with lather, sweat pouring down into the bright red neckerchief tied loosely around his sunburned neck. The hot, blinding sun reflected off the Texas Ranger badge pinned to his chest. The six men he was chasing disappeared behind a cluster of large boulders, and moments later a rifle shot rang out with a resounding crack as it penetrated the air. The giant slug slammed into the center of Buck's chest.

"Well, I'll be a goddamn som'bitch!" Buck said, rubbing his chest as he got up from the office floor and dusted himself off.

CHAPTER 16

No one called Irving (not Irv, not Holly, Irving) Hollister and Beaumont (you can call me Bo) Clayton Redneck and Watermelon in their presence, or even within earshot. Irving stood six feet two and weighed two hundred and thirty pounds. He had pleasant blue eyes, thin sandy hair, and no discernible neck. Bo was shorter by an inch, a rail-thin, medium-complected black man. His green eyes could be piercing, hostile, or happy, but you could never determine his moods by looking there. He could pinch off a rattlesnake's head without changing expression.

But their dissimilarities ended there. Redneck and Watermelon disliked everybody, and no one was ever sure if they even cared for each other. All criminals were dirt bags, pukes, or scumbags, and people in general were assholes. Although they could be surprisingly considerate and courteous in day-to-day dealings, their true feelings appeared at the slightest provocation. They just wouldn't tolerate the slightest bit of abuse from anyone.

The two had come together years before when they were routinely assigned to work as partners in the robbery detail. Their arrest rate was phenomenal, but it soon became obvious that pairing them was like mixing pure chlorine with dry acid. In most detective teams some semblance of balance exists, and day to day the cooler head usually prevails. But there was no balance with Bo and Irving. There was one way—their way—and they always agreed. They didn't care for petty police procedures and trivial details like paperwork. The only form that held their interest was the arrest report to be filled out when they put the puke or pukes in jail. Only two people knew all the details of what occurred before an arrest, and anyone who wanted those details had to ask Bo and Irving, who might or might not have something to say. In the courtroom they had terrible memories. They simply couldn't always recall the explicit details that they were expected to know. And they knew only one way to get information: go to the logical source and demand it, extort it, do anything but kill for it, but never stop short of threatening death to get it. They had to be separated, and, like an expensive drink, mixed only on special occasions.

Bo and Irving rarely displayed any mutual affection in public. One Christmas Bo gave Irving a book entitled *How To Get Along With Blacks*. On New Year's Day, which was also Bo's birthday, Irving gave it back with the word *Blacks* crossed out and replaced with *Niggers*. On the inside of the front cover he wrote, "To my favorite New Year's Nigger Baby, love, Irving."

On another occasion Irving wore a coonskin cap to work, explaining that he wanted to "feel closer to Bo's people."

The one and only time they were known to have socialized together occurred after they had a fight one afternoon in the detective division. For reasons unknown, they punched each other out, shook hands afterward, and agreed to have a beer at the end of shift. Halfway through their seventh Coors, some poor, unknowing soul said something about "the fucking pigs in this city," and minutes later the bar was *cleaned out*. The windows were shattered. The tables, chairs, and barstools were scattered in the street. Most of the liquor bottles were shot up into piles of glass gravel. And the bartender was flat on his back with the barrel of a forty-five automatic down his throat, choking out a promise that he'd never tell—and he never did. But the story did get around, and when it got around to Buck, he gave them both a year of purgatory working as tier guards in the main jail.

Captain Ernie Ratfern was a cop's cop, with a record second to none, though he didn't look the part. His short bowlegs were totally out of proportion to his body. He looked like a six-foot walking torso.

When Captain Ratfern walked up behind Watermelon, Bo was sitting at his desk and talking on the phone. His coat was off, exposing two forty-five automatics in shoulder holsters, one under each arm. The woman on the other end of the line was so irate that Bo could feel the heat coming through the receiver, burning his ear. "But ma'am, I can't help you," he pleaded.

"That's the trouble with you cops! When you wanna throw my kid in jail, you have all the time in the world, but when somebody complains, you suddenly run out of time."

"If you want to complain, ma'am, you have to call internal affairs. I can give you the number."

"Internal affairs, my ass! I've been passed from one jackass to another, and now you're goin' to listen to me whether you like it or not!"

"Ma'am, could I ask you a couple of questions first?"

"Okay, but then you're going to hear me out. Do you understand that?"

"Of course, ma'am," Bo replied. "Now, my first question is, do you have any idea who you're talking to?"

"No, and I don't give a shit! I don't care if you're the president of the United States."

"Very good. Now my second question, ma'am," Bo said extra politely, "is, do you recall what number you dialed to get me?"

"Hell, no! What goddamn difference does that make?"

"Well, then," Bo said, his green eyes flaming, "it's been nice talking with you, and FUCK YOU VERY MUCH!" He slammed down the phone with great joy. "That honky asshole, that fucking cunt," he mumbled to himself.

"How do you know she was a honky asshole and a fucking cunt?" Captain Ratfern's voice boomed behind him. "I've got your ass this time, Bo. After fifty goddamn complaints. I finally caught you."

"You ain't got shit, Cap'n," sneered Watermelon. "You come walkin' over here to give me some rotten-ass job for the *Sher'ff*," he mimicked Buck, "and then tell me you got my ass. Horseshit!"

"How do you know I've got an assignment from the sheriff, wise guy?"

"Because it's the *only* time, except quittin' time, that you walk out of that office with a smile."

Ratfern glared at Watermelon for a moment. "Well," he said, coughing and clearing his throat, "where's Irving? I might as well give it to you both at the same time."

"Oh, bullshit, Cap'n. Give us what? One word—Crotch! I read this morning's paper," he said. "IRVING!"

Within seconds, Irving strolled out of the robbery detail office and walked slowly up to Bo's desk. "Got something for us, Captain? Wouldn't be Crotch now, would it?" His smile broke into a grin.

Ratfern stared at Irving and didn't say a word.

"Piece of cake, Captain," Irving laughed. "Yes, sir. Sponge cake."

Redneck and Watermelon knew it was coming. They were only surprised that it took so long. They knew what they were going to do and how they were going to do it, and by late the next morning, they had an old panel truck and all the gear they needed—one sawed-off, pump shotgun with a pistol grip. Irving always drove, and Bo did most of the talking. Years before, Bo fell into the habit of altering his speech and mannerisms to fit whatever social situation he was in, mimicking those around him. It was so casual that no one noticed, not even Bo. At one point, his wife wasn't sure if she'd married a college professor or an Arkansas mule skinner; it drove her half crazy, but it was often helpful to Bo.

Shortly before noon, Irving picked up Bo at his house, and they headed for Swish Alley, their equipment covered with an old hand towel and lying on the seat between them. Irving, who had donned faded blue jeans and an old blue work shirt, let out a hoot and then covered his face with his hands when he saw Bo in skin-tight black slacks, a white satin dress shirt, and a bright red bandana rolled up and tied around the top of his head. Bo was going to wear one gold earring but wasn't sure which ear to put it on, so he wore two. They were an incongruous, totally believable pair.

Swish Alley was the cops' name for a small but well-known park in eastern Sacramento County that gays, both local and transient, used as a gathering and meeting place. Redneck and Watermelon arrived before noon, parked a half block away, and watched the increasing activity in silence. After about thirty minutes, Irving tapped Bo on the shoulder.

"Hey, Bo, what about that over there?" He pointed in the direction of the driveway entering the park.

"Huh? Where?" Bo moved in his seat to see around a tree that was in his line of sight. Then he spotted the young man standing on the grass about ten feet from the drive. He was tall and thin, sported long blond hair, and wore a powder-blue jump suit with matching patent leather belt and shoes and a blue and white polkadot scarf around his neck. "Hmmm, hmmm. Yeah, okay, let's go."

Irving stopped the truck on a dime, and Bo, smiling, with his earrings sparkling in the bright sunlight and his arm hanging outside the window, said, "Hey, baby, what's happenin'?"

The young man, smiling, strolled over to the truck and leaned against the door, inches from Bo's watermelon smile. "Hi, guys. Looking to party?"

Bo moved his right hand up and gently rubbed the back of the young man's neck, grinning as he slipped his left hand under the towel and firmly grasped the shotgun.

"Yeah, baby, we're looking to party big-time," Bo said as he snapped a vise grip on the back of the young man's neck, pulled his head through the open window, and rammed the shotgun into his Adam's apple. "Don't move, cocksucker, and don't pass out or I'll turn your head into hamburger."

"Wh-wh-what d-do you want?" he stuttered, grimacing from the pain radiating through his neck.

"We're with the sheriff's cocksucker patrol. Where you from, cocksucker?"

"Frisco!" cried the young man.

Bo eased the grip on his neck.

"Shit!" Bo said, looking at Irving and then back at the young

138

man. "Do you come up here often, sweet lips?" Bo sneered. "Know a lot of the people around here?"

"Ye-yeah, sure."

"Anybody here know all the other faggots and weirdos in town?" Bo stared into his blinking eyes.

"Ye-yes," he cried, "I think so."

"Do you want to live or die?" Bo asked very matter of factly.

"Live, oh yes. Yes, sir, I wanna live!"

"That's good, cocksucker, 'cause there's two people we don't wanna have to kill," Bo smiled, "you and the guy you send over here."

"The guy I send over?" the young man questioned.

"That's right," Bo said. "You're gonna find me the smartest dick licker in the park and send him over here. And if everything goes right we won't ever kill either one of you."

"Wha' . . . what do you mean?"

"Every once in a while we kill a faggot or two," Bo said, very sincerely, "and if you and the guy you send over here do as we say, we'll never kill either one of you. Look at it this way—you're saving a life." Bo smiled.

"Tha-that's a he-he-hell of a deal," the young man forced a weak smile. "Take you up on that!"

"Good. Good," Bo grinned, dropping his hand from the young man's neck, leaving the shotgun in place. "Now, hand me your wallet." The young man complied and Bo handed it to Irving. Irving went through the wallet, removing the driver's license and two photographs, one of a suntanned, naked muscle beach boy and the other of the young man hugging the muscle beach boy. Then he gave the wallet back to Bo, who passed it to the young man. "Now, you go find the most knowledgeable, intelligent cocksucker out there and send him to us. And then you go back to Frisco and keep your mouth shut, and you'll get this stuff back later. If you don't keep your mouth shut, we'll hunt you down and that other penis erectus in your pictures, and kill you both."

"Okay. Okay, I'll do as you say," the young man said, looking ill. "Like I said, hell of a deal."

The young man walked slowly away from the truck, regaining his composure. He wandered around the park for a few minutes, then sat down on the grass next to a dark-haired man about the same age. A minute later the second young man got up and started walking toward the truck.

"Looks like a piece of cake," said Irving with a smile.

"Ooh, and so pretty," cracked Bo.

"Hello," the second young man said, politely. "Want a party, huh?" He smiled broadly.

"Yeah, baby. What's the happenin's?" Bo grinned as he opened the door. "Hop in." Bo pulled the back of his seat forward and the second young man climbed into the back of the truck. He stood on his knees, facing Bo and resting his left arm on the back of Irving's seat. Bo turned toward him, his left arm draped over the back of his seat, his right hand moving toward the towel. Bo put his left hand on the second young man's shoulder, rubbed it gently, and smiled. He smiled back at Bo. "Are you a faggot?" asked Bo.

The young man stared at Bo for a second, knowing he made a mistake by getting into the truck. He swallowed hard. "I'm gay, if that's what you mean."

"Gay. I'm gay, too," Bo said, forcing a giggle, "but I ain't no goddamn faggot! You are a faggot," he yelled, putting that viselike grip on the young man's shoulder, bringing the shotgun over the top of the seat, into his chest. "You think this would fit in your asshole, asshole?" The young man trembled and shook his head.

Irving switched on the ignition, pulled out of the park, and began an aimless drive. Bo released his grip but kept the shotgun against his chest. "From now on," Bo said, "your name *is* Faggot!"

"Wh-wh-what do you want?"

"Do you give *head*?" Bo asked, ignoring his question.

"Y-y-yes," Faggot said. "W-w-want o-one?"

"How many a day?" Bo smiled.

"O-o-oh o-on a g-good day, maybe three," Faggot said, "sometimes four. Wh-wh-who are you?"

"We're the sheriff's faggot patrol," Bo said with a smile. "We kill cocksuckers. That's our job!"

"Ohhhh. Ohhh, ohhh, ohhh," Faggot cried. "Damn! Damn, oh damn, damn, damn."

"Give me your wallet, Faggot." Bo flipped through it and removed the driver's license.

"Wh-wh-wh-wh—aw shit!—are you gonna kill me?"

"You know those bodies they find floating in the river? The ones with no heads?" Faggot nodded and started to cry. "Well, we put 'em there," Bo grinned, "and that's where you're goin' . . ."

"AAaahhhhh, aahhh, no. *Please no!* I'll do anything—anything you want."

Bo and Irving looked at each other, expressionless. "Anything?" asked Bo.

"Anything. J-j-just t-tell me what you want."

"Well, Faggot," said Bo, "we're lookin' for a weirdo. A particular weirdo. He's about your size, wears a bright green windbreaker, drinks Dr. Pepper, and collects crotches out of women's pantyhose. You know any dudes like that?"

"No. Nobody like that."

"Then find him, Faggot! You've got three days."

"F-f-f-find him? How?" Faggot began to cry again.

"You're weird and all your faggot friends are weird, and you and all your weird friends are going to check every weird hangout in town until you find this weirdo. But nobody is to know why. That's our little secret. You can keep a secret, can't you, Faggot?"

Faggot nodded. "I'll t-t-try. I-I-I mean yes. I'll find him and I'll keep the secret."

Irving turned the truck around and headed back to the park.

"Remember, Faggot, three days," Bo cautioned. "We'll be back in three days. Same time, same place."

"Right. Yes, sir. Three days," Faggot mumbled as he stepped down from the truck and accepted his wallet from Bo, minus the driver's license. As Faggot walked away, Bo and Irving studied each other's faces for a moment.

"Something bothering you?" Irving asked.

"Yeah. Be right back." Bo jumped from the truck and ran over to Faggot, who was about twenty yards away.

Irving watched as they talked. Moments later Faggot took something out of his wallet and handed it to Bo. When Bo got back in the truck he laid it on the seat next to Faggot's driver's license. It was a color photograph of a matronly woman and on the bottom half was written, "To my wonderful son, Love, Mother."

"What's that for?"

"Insurance," Bo said, looking away.

"Insurance? What kind of insurance is that?" There was a moment of silence. "Well," Irving smirked, "is it some kind of secret?"

Bo continued to look out the windshield. "I told him that if he snitched us off and didn't do exactly what we told him to do,

that we would not only cut his head off, but that—we would—
that picture of his mother would be used for toilet paper."

There was a prolonged period of silence. "You didn't," Irving
said, staring at Bo. "Not his *mother*. You didn't use his mother?
Did you?" They stared at each other for a moment, then Bo forced
a smile. A weak, sick smile. "Disgusting," Irving mumbled to
himself as he drove out of the park.

CHAPTER 17

WHEN STONEY DECIDED to try to employ Topper Vance, he knew that he was scraping the bottom of the honey bucket. But he also knew that Topper was *the* photographer, par excellence.

Topper grew up with a camera in his hand, and his first job was taking babies' pictures in the corner of a supermarket. Shortly thereafter, he graduated to taking babies' pictures in a studio, and from there to the *Bunion*, where he worked for several years. His last job before becoming a blackmailer was with the CIA, where he polished off his training for both of his professions. For two years, Topper traveled around the world for the CIA, and when he quit, he stole every piece of photographic equipment he could get his hands on. Topper was equipped to take any kind of picture—any time, any place.

Topper had a very successful "business" photographing people where they didn't belong. He specialized in couples exiting motel rooms and often scored a double-header—two "clients" from one picture. Married men dating other men's wives proved especially lucrative. He maintained his hit list by hanging around

145

bars, developing "friendships," and learning who was dating who and if the whos belonged to someone else. His clients never knew who he was, and many continued to drink with him long after their payments began. Topper used a fictitious name and always maintained two post office boxes at different locations. He gave the client one address and had the mail forwarded to the other, ruling out the opportunity for surveillance by a disgruntled client.

Topper wasn't greedy for a lump sum payment. Like other successful businessmen, he accepted small monthly payments, and by the end of his first year, more than a hundred clients were paying him an average of forty dollars a month. If Topper was collecting from a husband and wife at the same time, which was not uncommon, he granted a slight discount from his normal fee. He had a heart the size of a washtub.

Of course, everything that Topper made was tax free. When he left the CIA, he had had himself "killed." As far as the government was concerned, he was dead.

In the hills northeast of Sacramento, D.C., Topper had built a little two-room, two-story cabin on the top of a hill, cleared all of the trees for one hundred yards around, and thrown up an electric cyclone fence around the perimeter. Inside the fence were two Dobermans that he had raised on raw meat laced with human blood, which he paid a janitor at the blood bank to steal for him. Topper's blood was type O, and whenever he got a jug of it, he spiked it with Louisiana hot sauce before giving it to the dogs. They ran from type O, but developed a lion's thirst for all other types. Topper kept them in a cage until they were properly conditioned, then turned them loose inside the fence.

Stoney alone knew what Topper was doing, and that knowledge came to him quite by accident. When one of his closest friends got on the hit list and showed the "impossible" pictures to Stoney, it didn't take him long to figure out who took them. Topper destroyed the negatives and was forever grateful to Stoney for not revealing his secret, which would not only have destroyed his business but also sent him to federal prison for most of the remaining years of his life. And besides that, Stoney had type O blood. He could visit without fear of being devoured by the Dobermans.

Stoney made several trips to Topper's cabin, and every time he did, the Dobermans ran like Pavlov's dogs for a long drink of water. Topper didn't have a phone, and it took eight trips before Stoney finally found him at home.

Topper turned off the electricity and greeted Stoney at the gate in a far corner of the perimeter fence. The Dobermans couldn't bear having two type O people around. They wolfed down a gallon of water apiece and then hid under the house, where they couldn't see or smell Topper and Stoney.

Stoney and Topper shook hands just inside the gate, and Topper locked it behind them. Stoney glanced around the barren hilltop encircled by the twelve-foot-high cyclone fence topped off with barbed wire.

Stoney scratched the top of his head. "Topper," he wondered, "why in the world are you living up here like this?"

Topper was thirty-six years old. He had dark hair, and his blue eyes sparkled when he talked. "Oh, hell, Stoney, it's real nice now that I got the top cleared off. I can see for a mile down the hill. Got a good clear field of fire."

"Field of fire?"

"Yeah. Then I got the fence, and if they make it past the fence, I got the dogs. I can pick off the ones with type O blood." Stoney stared at him, bewildered. Topper continued, "And I got a good three-sixty-degree field of view from inside the house, too.

Got one room up and one down, with windows in every wall, and I got a fifty-caliber or a B.A.R. mounted in every window. Yeah, Stoney boy, I'm ready for 'em when they come."

"Just who are *they*, Topper?"

"The Commies, Stoney." Topper grimaced. "The Central Americans . . . Mexicans . . . niggers, and white liberals. Liberals, hell, they're all Commies. I fought with the Contras toward the end . . . had Ortega in my sights once. Should've shot the son-of-a-bitch. Then the politicians caved in—the bunch of crooks—goddamned left-wing pinko bastards. Now Central America is solid red. Mexico will fall next, and then they'll start pouring over the border, with the government troops and Russians helping 'em. But we'll be ready."

"You left out the Chinese, Topper," Stoney said sarcastically.

"Naw, not yet, Stoney," he said. "That's still a few years down the road. And besides that, I think I could talk to those people—negotiate."

Stoney let the subject drop. He hadn't seen Topper for more than two years, and this was all new to him. After they walked into the house, Topper locked the door. Then he proceeded to look out each downstairs window and test fire a short burst from the guns as he went—cartridges flying from the breeches, acrid smoke wafting through the room.

As Stoney looked around, he was further amazed. Stacked in one corner was a huge pile of bundled-up greenbacks. "My God, Topper! How much money is that?"

"Oh, I'm not really sure anymore, Stoney." Topper glanced at the bundles and scratched his chin. "I'd guess about a million and a half."

"A million five?" Stoney swallowed hard and then stared at

the photographer. "Topper, that kind of money should be in a bank."

"Aw, Stoney," Topper said, shaking his head, "you can't trust those banks, and besides I *have* to deal in cash." He smiled. "See, Stoney, I'm legally dead. When I left the CIA, they killed me— on paper of course. I was executed by a firing squad in Iran. Terrible tragedy." He laughed.

"I don't believe it. Or you," Stoney said, shaking his head. "What in the world are you going to do with all this dough?"

"Oh, you can't believe all the work that's got to be done, Stoney," Topper said, grimacing again. "I've got to armor-plate all these walls . . ."

"What!"

". . . and my neighbors, the allies," he continued, "we've got three more hills I have to help fortify."

"Oh God, Topper. You mean there are more people around here just like you?"

"Oh, yeah, Stoney. We're in pretty good shape." Now Topper was smiling. "We've secured the best three hills in this part of the country. And after they're fortified, we have to start on some barracks, a P.X., and . . ."

"Enough! Stop!" Stoney screamed. "I can't take it anymore Let's just visit and get to what I'm here for." His stomach was churning, and as soon as he cut Topper off, he started feeling better. "I need a big favor, and you owe me, Topper."

"Yeah, I sure do, Stoney. I'll do whatever I can. You just name it."

"Are you still *working*, Topper? Do you still have your equipment?"

"Oh, I've got my stuff, Stoney. Wouldn't ever get rid of that

But I'm not working much. Don't like to leave the hill except to buy ammunition and supplies, and I have to go a long way for them at times. Besides, all my clients pay good. Hardly ever have to send a reminder anymore, and I've got a whole year's supply of pictures that I haven't even used yet." Topper cackled at the thought.

"Topper, I want you to try to get some pictures of the governor in his apartment at night."

"The governor?" Topper said, surprised.

"Yeah, but don't ask me for the details," Stoney pleaded. "It's a long story. Look, I need pictures of who he's entertaining. It might take a while, but I've got to know."

"Entertaining," laughed Topper. "You mean fuckin', don't you?"

"That's right, Topper. His apartment is upstairs facing the street, but there's some tall palm trees outside. Ever climb a palm tree for a picture, Topper?"

"No, I sure haven't, Stoney. I thought I'd done it all. Between the CIA and the business, I haven't missed much. I'll have to survey it and see if it can be done. I'll check it this evening and let you know."

"Thanks," Stoney said, relieved. "Just one last thing, Topper. This isn't a deal. It's a favor—to me. You can't use these pictures in your business. They're mine. Agreed?"

"You got it, Stoney," Topper smiled. "My word is my bond." And with Topper it was.

Topper called Stoney late that night. "Looks good, friend," he said. "I'll go to work just as soon as I get back from Fresno."

"Fresno? What the heck did you lose in that place?" Stoney laughed.

"I've got a friend down there with a yard full of palm trees. Going to practice for three or four days."

"Can't you do that right here in D.C.?"

"Can't trust *anybody* up here, Stoney."

"Good night, Topper."

"Good night, Stoney."

CHAPTER 18

O<small>N THE MORNING</small> that it happened, Buck was practicing his hangman's knot and feeling very depressed; Stoney was still in bed, thinking about Topper Vance and his fortress, nursing a headache; Axel was finishing off his second quart of prune juice; J.J. was going through his morning ritual, bowing to the picture of Daniel Ortega that hung on the east wall of his office; and Red Ainess was composing the rough draft of a "love" letter from J.J. to Toni Mandrocci.

At approximately 9:40, the red phone in Red Ainess's capitol office began ringing. He picked it up on the third ring. "Ainess here."

"Red, this is Axel," his voice squeaking with a mix of excitement and distress. "It happened! Red, it *happened!*"

"Calm down, Axel, for crying out loud. What's *it*? What happened?"

"*IT,* Red! *IT HAPPENED! SAN FRANCISCO FELL INTO THE OCEAN!*"

Ainess stood silent for a moment, confused and then disgusted. "You're sick, Axel."

"Red!" Axel cried, "I'm not bullshitting you. It really happened. About five minutes ago. It just came over the wire."

"Okay. Okay, Axel," Red said patronizingly. "Whatever you say. I'll be in touch."

Red was laughing and shaking his head when he dialed the red phone at the governor's branch office in San Francisco. But he got nothing. No busy signal. Nothing. He dialed the operator.

"Operator. May I help you?" she chirped.

"Yes, operator, this is Red Ainess of the governor's office, and I'm trying to reach area code 415-969-6969, but I'm not getting anything. Nothing."

"What city is that, sir?"

"San Francisco."

"One moment, please." A minute passed. Red could hear the sound of papers shuffling. "I'm sorry, sir, but there is no such number and no such city. Thank you for calling Pacific Bell."

Red turned pale. In his mind's eye he saw Buck dressed in a long white robe, laughing. He ran to his wastepaper basket and retched. Then he ran to J.J.'s office. As he ran through the door, the secretary put up his hand like a traffic cop and then moved his finger to his mouth, indicating for Red to be quiet. The inner door to J.J.'s office was closed. "It's that time of the morning, Red. It should only be a few more minutes."

Red sat down. Five minutes later the door opened, and J.J. stepped out. "Red, you look ill," he said. "Is something wrong?"

"It fell in, sir. San Francisco fell right into the goddamned ocean, just like Buck Mullins said it would."

"That's nice, Red."

"It's true!" Red cried. "Axel called me. Then I tried to call the red phone and got nothing. I called the operator. She said 'no such number, no such city.' "

"Holy cow," moaned J.J. "That means I've lost the endorsement of two major newspapers."

J.J. sat down, glassy-eyed. Then he too had a vision of the prophet Mullins, and he passed out.

San Francisco fell into the ocean at exactly 9:34:32 A.M. according to all official reports. Witnesses reported that there was absolutely no warning and no noise. The city simply broke off and silently but swiftly slid into the ocean. There was no flotsam and jetsam, and no bodies were found. Divers reported that the water was very muddy but there was no sign or evidence of the city. The Golden Gate Bridge and the bridge connecting Oakland and Yerba Buena Island remained intact, but the San Francisco portion of the Bay Bridge was gone. There was absolutely no physical evidence found to prove that the city ever existed.

At one o'clock, a revived J.J. called a meeting with Axel and Red Ainess. "Red, how's that San Francisco thing going?"

"No sign of any survivors, Governor," Red said soberly. "It's gone. Everything's gone—like it never existed."

"Oh. Okay," J.J. said very matter of factly. "Well now, Axel, how are we going to turn this thing around? How are we going to discredit that slimebag sheriff?"

"I don't know, Governor. I have no idea."

J.J. leaned forward and pointed a finger at the newspaperman. "Listen, Axel, you get a reporter over there to interview him. Make him look like the idiot he is. Just like you did last time. Just get him talking. He'll take care of the rest."

"He won't talk to anybody, Governor. He's playing it smart. Reporters are here from all over the state. By tonight, there'll be newshounds here from all over the country. And he won't let one of them near the place. He's already got Buster and his SWAT team up on the roof, ready to drop tear gas on anyone who gets too close. He thinks he's a prophet, the people think he's a prophet, and he's not going to do or say anything to change that. He won't talk to anybody."

"We could send in the National Guard," Red Ainess chimed in, "and drag his ass out of there."

"No," J.J. cautioned, "that didn't work for Pontius Pilate, and it won't work for us. That would just make a bigger hero out of him."

"And things could get worse, J.J.," Axel said with a frown. "I heard that he's got Redneck and Watermelon out trying to catch Crotch. If they do, Buck'll be a god around here. Of course, if those two maniacs screw up, Buck will be right back where he started from."

"Well," said J.J., scratching his cheek, "then let us all hope and pray that they kill some poor innocent slob."

When Buck first heard the news, he couldn't believe it. For an hour he paced around his office, wondering what it meant. He considered changing his name to Elijah or Moses but thought better of it and decided to wait for the "message" before doing anything. He refused to see or talk to anyone, but by the end of that first hour, he returned to earth. When he did, he concentrated on how to keep a good thing going. Nevertheless, he was haunted by the feeling that it might possibly be true—he just might be a prophet. Only time would tell. In the meantime he wouldn't grant interviews to anyone.

At eleven o'clock, his private phone rang. In a deep voice Buck answered, "Hello."

"Buck. This is Stoney," he said, excited. "Did you hear? It happened! It actually happened! It fell in! Can you believe it?"

"Yes, Stoney, my son," Buck said very slowly. "I received word just over an hour ago. The Lord giveth and the Lord taketh away. There is no greater power!"

"Buck, are you all right? You're not yelling or cheering or cussing."

"It is not a time for those things, Stoney, my son. I have much to consider, much to contemplate. My life has been elevated to a much higher plane of responsibility. To a greater power. A greater calling."

"Whoa, Buck. Wait a minute, big guy. You don't really think . . . no . . . oh, not that! Do you, Buck?"

"Do I what, my son?"

"Oh God, I think you do," moaned Stoney. "I don't believe it. Topper Vance yesterday and now you. I can't take it anymore—goddarnit! Goodbye, Buck. Talk to you later . . . I guess."

Reporters and others continued to flood Brenda with calls, but Buck wouldn't talk to anybody. He remained in his office with the door closed, looking at his plaques, then his photos, then his saddle, trying to discern a message. Biblical scholars swarmed into Sacramento, D.C., eager to investigate Buck's background, hoping to find Judaic links in his ancestry, but Buck especially didn't want to see them.

Buck did grant one request, however, just to test himself. The lady with the diplegic invalid canary had been calling all day, wanting to bring in her pet so that Buck could touch it with his healing powers, in the hope that his wing feathers might grow. Buck allowed that she could come in at four o'clock.

Buck gently cradled the little canary in his massive hands for

157

a few moments; then he told the lady to take it home and wait in prayer. She left the building in tears and smiles, happier than she'd been in months. But she stumbled forward on the sidewalk, and the canary popped from her hands and rolled like a ball into the street, where a Mack truck crushed it into something resembling twenty-pound bond canary paper. In a state of shock, the woman peeled her pet off the street and marched into Buck's office.

A deputy at the public counter, in the lobby, saw what happened and called Buck to let him know she was coming and gave him all the details.

"You're no prophet!" she screamed at Buck, dangling her former pet between thumb and forefinger. "Look at Harold!"

"Ah, yes, dear woman, but I did see it coming." He put his right hand gently on the top of her head and held Harold in his left. "When I held the little one in my hands, I knew then that it was doomed, but I couldn't tell you because there was no stopping it. Harold was in the hands of the higher power."

She looked about his office and noted that there was no way he could see the street. "Well, if you're a prophet, wise guy, tell me how it happened!"

Buck sighed. "Oh, dear woman, do you really want to relive those terrible moments?"

"Yes, Mister Prophet, I do!"

Buck handed the sheet of Harold back to the lady and brought both hands to his face, closing his eyes. "I see you leaving the building, and I see the truck coming. On the sidewalk, inexplicably, you stumble, and little Harold floats from your hands. He's in the air. He's flying for just a second. Then gravity gets him in her grasp, and he's falling to the ground. Now he's rolling, but he's unaware of the danger, happy for the exercise. But then the inevitable happens. His destiny. The right front wheel of a Mack truck flattens his little body and sends him—flying—toward heaven."

Buck removed his hands from his face and opened his eyes. The woman stood dumbfounded, the light of faith kindled in her sad eyes. When Buck looked at her, she dropped to her knees, kissed the tops of his boots, and hurried away.

After she had gone, Buck told Brenda, sweetly of course, to lock up and go home a little early. Then he walked over to the Texas Ranger saddle. He stood there for a moment looking toward the sky, took three deep breaths, and then mounted up.

When the mist and clouds cleared, there was Buck riding on the back of a young ass. He led a triumphal procession that wound its way through narrow streets teeming with people. And the people were laying down palm branches in his path.

CHAPTER 19

B O AND IRVING arrived at Swish Alley at the appointed time and parked in the same spot where they let Faggot out three days before. A few minutes later, Faggot approached the truck, walking very slowly and looking forlorn.

"He doesn't look too good," Irving moaned, negative thoughts drifting through his mind.

"Yeah," Bo agreed. "I was just thinking the same thing." Faggot stopped an arm's length away from the truck door, remembering the grip that Bo had put on his neck, and stared at the ground. "Well," asked Bo, "what good news do you have for us today, Faggot?"

"I don't know for sure," Faggot mumbled. "Maybe nothin', but there is a guy who hangs around Velma's, a lesbian place over in D.C. He's not gay—he's nothin'." He looked up at Bo. "If this isn't the guy, you gotta give me a little more time. Please?"

"We'll see. Anything else about 'im? What makes you think he's the guy?"

161

"He drinks Dr. Pepper almost constantly," Faggot said, perking up slightly. "Velma says he's kind of a mascot around there. We didn't see it, but she says he has a green jacket. He just doesn't wear it much in the summer."

"Thanks, Faggot. We'll be back in touch."

Faggot looked at Bo for a moment, forlorn again. Then he turned and walked slowly away, dragging his feet. Bo and Irving sat looking at each other. "Give me the stuff," Bo said, thrusting out his open hand. Irving handed him Faggot's driver's license and the picture of his mother.

Bo caught up with Faggot, put his arm gently on his shoulder, and handed him the driver's license and picture. They talked briefly, and as they parted, Faggot was smiling.

"Let's go," said Bo as he climbed into the truck.

"Well, what did you tell 'im?"

"Nothin'. Just nothin'!" Bo refused to look at Irving, who grinned as he fired up the truck and headed for Velma's.

Velma's was a little side-street bar in downtown Sacramento, D.C., that always did a brisk business from noon on, but when Bo and Irving arrived and parked across the street, they saw a black wreath hanging on a padlocked front door. Bo ran across the street to read the gold lettering on the wreath.

"Well, what does it say?" Irving asked as Bo climbed back into the truck.

"It's in memory of some dude named Harold, whoever the hell he is. A note says they'll be open tomorrow. Let's pack it in and start back here tomorrow."

"Naw, let's wait for the beat cop to come around. He oughta know something about this guy."

After what seemed like an eternity, a huge Sacramento, D.C., policeman came strolling down the sidewalk, munching on a hunk of jack cheese. He looked eighteen months pregnant, and his pants, which were six inches too short, exposed not only his drooping white socks but a good portion of his hairy legs. His old gun was covered with at least a pound of rust. When he was parallel with the truck across the street, Irving whistled and flashed his badge. The cop jaywalked over to the truck and stood in the street next to Irving's door.

"Hi, there," he greeted, raising one big paw. "Jerry. Jerry Carnes." He put the paw out to Irving.

Irving shook his hand. "Irving Hollister. This is my partner, Bo Clayton."

"Nice meeting you, *Irv*," Jerry said, smiling. Irving grimaced. "You, too, Bo. What can I do for you?"

"Been on this beat long?" asked Irving.

"Oh, 'bout twenty-three years is all," Jerry laughed.

Irving smirked. "Know anything about a guy that hangs around Velma's drinking Dr. Pepper?"

"Oh, hell yeah," answered Jerry, very matter of factly. "That's Sloth you're talkin' about. He's here most every day, rain or shine, suckin' down gallons o' that shit."

"Do you know anything else about him? His real name or where he might live?"

"Naw. He's just another *character* on this beat. Got a lot of those around here." Jerry laughed and his big belly shook.

"Yeah, you sure do!" said Irving, looking Jerry up and down. "Ever see him wearing a bright green windbreaker?"

"Oh, hell yeah! Even in hot weather sometimes. Like I said— a real character."

"Have you ever heard of Crotch, Jerry?" Irving asked.

"Oh, hell yeah!" chortled the cop. "But he ain't ever hit *my* beat, by God! No sirree."

163

"Have you ever checked out this Sloth? Turn his name in to our dicks? He fits, the way it sounds."

"Oh, hell no," Jerry frowned, "not that character. Hell no!" He laughed, shaking his head and his belly.

Irving started up the truck and put it in gear. "Thanks a lot, Jerry. Keep up the good work," he said. Then he floored the pedal.

"One of D.C.'s finest," Bo mumbled. "He'd make a good chief."

When Bo and Irving returned late the next morning, Sloth was leaning against the front of the building, slugging down a can of Dr. Pepper. They parked half a block away. Just as Irving turned off the motor, Sloth walked into the bar. A short time later, he emerged with a six-pack of Dr. Pepper and shuffled down the sidewalk.

Bo and Irving looked at each other. Then Bo said, "Let's just creep along with the creep and see where he goes."

Sloth led them through town, over the American River and into north Sacramento, D.C., drinking Dr. Pepper and littering the street with his empties. Bo and Irving, in the truck, crept and parked as he shuffled along. Finally, after an hour and a half, Sloth ditched his last empty on a dried-up lawn and walked into a house.

"What a fuckin' dump!" said Irving, stating the obvious. "Must be on welfare. What now, Bo? What do you think?"

"I don't know. He doesn't have the jacket on. Must be in the house. Let's wait and see if there's anybody else around before we try and take him."

Five minutes later, Sloth came out the front door with a can of Dr. Pepper in his hand and a six-pack tucked under his arm. He started to shuffle off in the direction of Velma's.

"Oh, shit!" Irving moaned. "Not again."

Bo grabbed a portable radio from under the seat and clipped it to his belt. He opened the door and said, "You follow the genius, and when I call, grab him and bring him back here."

"What are you going to do? Or should I ask?"

Bo just smiled. Irving returned the smile and then drove away as Bo walked casually across the street and up to the front door of Sloth's house. When no one answered his knock, he knocked harder. As he knocked the third time with his right hand, he turned the doorknob with his left. It was unlocked. He slipped through the doorway and locked the door behind him.

Damn place smells like a sewer, he thought as he started to check the house. The kitchen had two refrigerators—one with a smattering of foodstuffs and the other choked with prune juice and Dr. Pepper. One bedroom was littered with dirty clothes and empty prune juice bottles, while another was littered with dirty clothes and empty Dr. Pepper cans.

When Bo opened the closet door in the second room, his green eyes caught fire. Clothes were piled on the closet floor. The lone item on a hanger was a very bulky, bright green windbreaker. When Bo ripped it off the hanger, he discovered the reason for the bulk. Layers of sewn-together pantyhose crotches made up the liner. He whistled into his portable radio, placed the jacket on a chair visible from the front door, and left the house, leaving the door unlocked. He waited for Irving across the street from the house.

When Irving drove up, he was laughing. Sloth was in the other seat, calmly downing a Dr. Pepper.

"What the hell's going on?" asked Bo. "What's so damn funny?"

"Just watch and listen," Irving laughed. "Hey, Sloth."

"Huh?" Sloth looked at Irving through half-opened eyes.

165

"How come they call you Sloth?"

"My dad gave that name to me. It's a Bible name, he says. I like it."

"Have you ever heard of Crotch?"

"Huh? Crotch. Who?" He took another sip.

"Do you cut crotches out of ladies' pantyhose?"

"Huh? Oh, yeah," Sloth smiled.

"What do you do with them?"

"I sew 'em inside my jacket. Makes me feel real good!"

"Enough, enough goddamnit!" Bo yelled, scowling. "We went through all that shit for this!" he scowled. "I'd like to get that fuckin' shrink, Dr. Fuckhead Wilson, and cut his nuts off, if he's got any. Fuckin' prick." Bo was fuming. Flames leaped from his eyes.

"Wait a minute, Bo," said his partner. "One more thing— just for *you*, Bo." He grinned and said, "Hey, Sloth, run in and get your jacket. Then bring it to me like a good boy."

Sloth jumped from the truck and returned seconds later with the jacket. He handed it to Irving. Irving looked at Bo and flashed a wide one.

"I've just got two questions," Bo said, still angry. "How did you know who had Dr. Pepper, and . . ."

"Oh, that was easy," Sloth said proudly. "Empties in the garbage cans."

"Brilliant! Now, why did you hurt the canary?"

Sloth frowned and studied the street. Bo asked him again. "That lady tricked me!" Sloth blurted out. "She had empties, but she only had RC in the fridge. I hate RC!"

"That certainly makes sense," said Bo. Now he too couldn't help but smile. He looked at Irving. "Well, let's get him downtown and get this bullshit over with."

By the time they got him into jail, they knew who they had: Dorkas Rodd, son of Axel Rodd, city editor of the *Bunion*. Bo called Buck.

"What? You got 'im! Axel's kid! Hot damn! Now here's what I want you to do," Buck went on, practically beside himself with joy. "Put that little bastard in chains and leg irons and have him ready for me in five minutes."

"But Sheriff, he's an imbecile." Bo moaned.

"I don't give a fuck, Clayton. Just do as I say!"

"Yes, sir, *Sher'ff*," said Bo, saluting the phone with his middle finger.

"Don't get smart with me, Clayton, or I'll have your ass!"

"Fuck you, *Sher'ff!*" Bo slammed the phone into its cradle.

With appropriate sweetness and urgency, Buck told Brenda to phone the *Bunion* and every radio and television station in town and let them know that *he* had captured Crotch and would be arriving with him at the back door of the department in thirty minutes.

Thirty-five minutes later, a patrol car pulled up to the rear door of the department, and Buck emerged from the back seat with Sloth in tow, trussed up in chains and leg irons. The sheriff looked into the clicking cameras and spoke into the microphones that eager reporters thrust in his direction. "It was one hell of a fight, folks. The worst I've experienced in my entire career. That's it. Thank you."

That was all they needed. Buck was not only a prophet but a courageous lawman. That night and throughout the next day, Buck's picture with that "Mad Dog Crotch" in tow was flashed around the state on every television station except KROK-TV and in every newspaper except the *Bunion*. Buck was riding a wave of mass popularity, and he was determined to ride it right over the top of J.J. and into the governor's office.

167

An hour after Buck made his brief statement, Sloth was in jail and Axel was on the phone, screaming his head off. "You rotten, worthless bastard, Mullins! You framed my kid, and I'm gonna have your ass!"

"How does it feel, Axel?"

"How does what feel, fuckhead?!"

"Having your nuts dangling from the end of a pitchfork!" Buck yelled, laughing uncontrollably.

"Goddamn you, Buck, you son of a bitch. I'll get you if it takes the rest of my life!"

"Fuck thou, Axel," Buck said calmly. "Fuck thou." Then he put the phone down very gently.

CHAPTER 20

TEN DAYS HAD PASSED since he'd talked with Topper, and Stoney was beginning to wonder if something had happened to him, like falling out of a palm tree and landing on a cop. The last time he'd talked to Buck was the day that San Francisco slid into the ocean and disappeared. Now, after seeing the pictures of Buck and Sloth, he decided to quit reading the newspapers and watching the news on television. He wanted the pictures, if there was anything to take pictures of, but whether he got the pictures or not, he knew what he was going to do.

At 9:30 P.M. Stoney's phone rang. It was Topper. "Darn, Topper, I was beginning to think something terrible happened, like your getting thrown in jail. Where you been?"

"Oh, hell, Stoney," answered Topper cheerfully, "I didn't have any problems like that. Not old Topper. I had to stay in Fresno a little longer than I planned. I found out that those waving palm trees made me seasick, so I tied myself to the top of one for a couple nights and slept up there, and that took care of that. Just gotta get used to those things."

"Did you get some pictures?"

169

"Oh, Stoney, let me tell you! I was beginning to think that nothin' was ever going to happen. After about the third night up there, I was about . . ."

"Topper, cut out the rundown. Did you get the pictures?"

"Did I get pictures? Let me tell you, Stoney, those boys love to play. I never saw such action." He was laughing. "But I don't really think that these are fit for publication."

"Was J.J. on top or on the bottom?"

"Oh, Stoney," Topper laughed again, "our governor is quite a boy. Quite a little romper. He was all over the place but I'd say mostly on the bottom. It's those other two that really cracked me up—especially the one with the wig and the lipstick smeared all over his face."

"Who are the other two?" Stoney asked, sounding disinterested. He figured one of them would be Red Ainess and really didn't care. He had the proof he wanted.

"I don't recognize either one, Stoney. One guy's a physical disaster. Looks like an inverted pear. And when he wasn't playing with J.J., he was guzzling prune juice."

"Prune juice?"

"Yeah, Stoney. He must've drunk five gallons of that stuff the night they had their party."

"My God, Topper, that's Axel Rodd! He's the city editor of the *Bunion*. Came to work at the paper years after you left."

"I'll be damned. Is that right! Well, Stoney, I can sure see why he has to play with boys. He's so damn sorry lookin' that he'd need a million in cold, hard cash to buy the worst piece of tail at Mustang."

"What about the other guy, Topper?" Stoney was beginning to get interested. "Tall with red hair?"

"Nope. This was a great big burly guy. Don't really know

170

what he looks like because of that wig and that lipstick. He does have some tattoos, though."

"Could you see what they were?"

"Hold on, I got a picture right here. Let me have a look. Yeah, okay. He's got 'Mother' tattooed over his right breast, 'Father' over the left, and what looks like a Texas flag on his right shoulder."

"A Texas flag," Stoney perked up.

"Yeah, and right under that is a name." Topper went silent, teasing Stoney.

"Okay, okay, Topper, you've had your fun. What is it?"

"Buster!" Topper roared with laughter. Stoney's stomach rose to his throat and nearly choked him. For a few seconds, he couldn't speak. Topper stopped laughing. "You all right, friend? Got quite a group here. Sure would make some fine clients."

"No, Topper! We've got an agreement."

"Just kidding, Stoney," said Topper, and he was. "You want these tonight?"

"No, that's all right. You can bring them by tomorrow afternoon. By then I'll be packed and ready to go."

"Go? Where to, Stoney boy?"

"First to L.A. to mail a set of your pictures to those three turkeys and another to Buck. Anybody who comes looking for me there will be looking for a long time. I'm heading home to good old sanity in Manhattan."

"Manhattan! Jesus, Stoney, that place is as bad as the one that just fell into the ocean."

"Manhattan, Kansas, Topper. Manhattan, Kansas."

Stoney stayed in Los Angeles just long enough to mail the pictures. When his adrenaline stopped racing through his blood and settled into an idle, he patted the dashboard of his old car and laughed. "Toto, let's go home."

CHAPTER 21

A T THE PRECISE moment that Stoney Gilson pulled into his driveway in Manhattan, Kansas, Red Ainess ambled into J.J.'s office for his daily 8 A.M. briefing and first cup of coffee. Stoney had dropped the pictures in the mail three days earlier. Now, even as he breathed a sigh of relief, happy to be safely home, his stomach began to churn as he visualized J.J., Axel, and Buck opening the envelopes and seeing the photos for the first time.

Red was in good spirits, smiling and whistling "Hail to the Chief" as he entered J.J.'s office, his cup dangling from his right index finger. The smiling and whistling stopped abruptly when he saw J.J., kneeling on a small red pillow on the floor. He was dressed in a white kimono with a red silk scarf tied around his forehead. Beside him lay a samurai sword and a double-edged dagger. J.J. was staring at the pictures of Jane Fonda, Daniel Ortega, and Kim Philby, laid out in a row before him, and mumbling unintelligibly.

173

Red quickly closed the door. "Wha' . . . what the hell are you doing?"

"Seppuku. I'm going to commit seppuku, and I'll need your help."

"Seppuku?"

"Seppuku! Hara-kiri. It's the honorable thing to do. You'll be my second. I'll use the cutting knife, and at the appropriate moment, you will decapitate me with the samurai sword. I understand it's relatively painless." J.J. picked up the sword and held it out to Red. "Here, you'd better take a couple of practice swings."

"Oh, shit! Have you lost your goddamn mind? What in God's name is this all about?"

"On my desk. Look on my desk," J.J. said in a low voice, continuing to stare at the pictures and beg for forgiveness.

Red picked up the stack of pictures on the desk and studied each one intently. "My God!" He threw down the last one and turned toward J.J. "Who? How? Jesus H. Christ!"

"Stoney Gilson," J.J. mumbled. "Came in this morning's mail. From Los Angeles."

Red, turning white, flopped down in J.J.'s desk chair and stared through the window at the capitol grounds. J.J. lay on his back and stared at the ceiling. Both of them had the same thought: J.J. would never be president of these United States.

"Such travail, Red. Such travail. I've worked so hard and given so much of myself to this great state, our sovereign democracy. I'm reminded of those famous words conceived and uttered by one of our greatest statesmen: 'Behold, I do not give lectures or a little charity. When I give, I give myself.' " J.J.'s eyes began to moisten.

"A *statesman* said that?"

"Yes," J.J. sighed. "Senator Joseph Biden. It was the closing

174

line of the farewell speech he delivered to the United States Senate. He gave me an autographed copy of the text. Signed it right in front of me. God! If only I could create such beautiful verse."

"J.J., he may have uttered it, but—I hate to pop your bubble—Walt Whitman created it. Biden stole every word."

"Oh?" J.J. frowned and fell silent, passing the sleeve of the kimono over his moist eyes.

The momentary quietude was shattered by Axel. "I don't give a good goddamn about no fuckin' briefing!" he boomed at the governor's secretary as he burst through the door and then slammed it shut. "What the hell?" Axel stared at J.J. for a moment, his hands on his hips. "Never mind. I don't wanna know." He turned to Red Ainess. "Well, I see you got the good news, too. Well, you can relax—a little. I just talked to that right-wing, radical fascist little prick Gilson. He's in Kansas for Chrissake, but I'll get him. Someday, somehow, I'm gonna get that son of a bitch for this."

"Okay, okay, Great White Father," said Red. "Just tell us your plan. Why is it that we can relax—a little?"

"He told me he's not sending them to anyone else. Just us and Buck."

"You believe him?"

"The little prick doesn't lie."

"What about Buck?"

"Buck? Hell, Buster's in the pictures. What can he say or do?"

"But Buster never *did* anything," J.J. chimed in. "All he ever did was watch. He never even took off his jockey shorts!"

"We know that," said Axel, "and that's what Buster will tell Buck. But who'd ever believe it? No, I think that Okie bastard is neutralized."

"But how will we ever know?" J.J. moaned. "We'll go crazy wondering."

"I'll tell you how," said Axel, reaching for the phone. After a verbal battle with Brenda, he got through to Buck. "Good morning, Sheriff Mullins. How are you this fine morning?"

"Oh, I'm just fine this fine morning, Mister Rodd. And how're you this fine morning?"

"Couldn't be better. Did you get your morning mail yet?"

"No, not yet. But I got a nice little package yesterday afternoon, you *cocksucker!*" Buck roared with laughter. "I got you som'bitches by the short hairs now!"

Axel turned crimson upon hearing the appellation. "How do you figure, Buck? You're forgetting who's in those pictures."

"I'm not forgettin' nothin', you prune-juice-suckin' fairy. All Buster ever did was watch. He told me so, and I could tell by the look on his sorry mug that the dumb shit wasn't lying. And for the record, *Miss* Rodd, Captain Buster Mullins was on assignment, working under cover. Just doin' his duty as an officer of the law."

"That's a goddamn lie and you know it!"

"Sure. I know it and you know it, but that's the official story if this thing ever gets out, and you, Miss Rodd, could never prove otherwise. Like I said, I've got you som'bitches by the short hairs. Now tell that dildo with ears that if he stands for reelection, every prick of a city editor in the state is gonna get a copy of those pictures."

"You asshole!" Axel bellowed, slamming down the phone.

"Well," smirked Red, "sure sounds like you've taken care of everything, Axel. I guess we can *really* relax now."

"Go to hell!"

"What did he say?" J.J. cried.

176

"Don't ask me nothin' right now. I've got to think." Axel began to pace the floor, his hands clasped behind his back. After a few minutes, he stopped and placed another call to Buck. "Look, Sheriff," he said after another skirmish with Brenda, "I think we'd better talk, man to man, eyeball to eyeball."

"Man to *man?*" Buck chuckled. "Don't you mean . . ."

"Cut the bullshit, Buck. I'll come over to *your* office, hat in hand. You can't beat that."

"Hmm . . . well, all right. I got nothin' to lose. Come on over. I'm waitin'."

"Axel, what in the hell are you going to do?" asked Red. "Grovel before that idiot?"

"Hey! You want an ironclad way out of this fuckin' mess, don't you? Well, I think I've got it, and if that Okie bastard goes for it, J.J.'ll have an open road to the White House."

Red glared at Axel. "What do you have in mind?"

"Don't ask. You're not going to like it, but I don't want to argue about it now. I'll be back after I'm finished with that gaping asshole." Axel turned on his heel and walked out the door.

When he returned, two hours later, Axel was smiling but looked nervous. Buck had bought the deal, but Axel was right— J.J. and Red didn't like it. Nevertheless, after an hour of heated discussion, they agreed that it was the only way to keep Buck quiet and off their backs.

J.J. slowly rose to his feet and rubbed his back. He was stiff from lying prone the entire morning. "My God! I can't believe this is happening to *me,*" he mumbled as he stumbled toward the wastepaper basket. He didn't make it. He lost his breakfast halfway there.

CHAPTER 22

EXCEPT FOR THE "terrorist" attack on J.J.'s residence, Sacramento, D.C., returned to relative normalcy, including the political scene, which became surprisingly inert. A series of explosions devastated the swaying palms in front of the governor's apartment house. In the process an excessive amount of plastic explosives was used, and the front of the building was also destroyed. J.J. was conveniently in southern California at the time, touring Reverse Punishment Crime Control Colonies. Though one reporter wanted to "allege" that a group of conspirators, "possibly" involving Sheriff Buck Mullins, was responsible for the attack, Red Ainess assured him that was not the case, and the story never ran. Finally, the *Bunion* put the matter to rest with a front-page editorial, after an "intensive investigation implicated the right-wing, fascist, capitalist" Republican National Committee.

Buck spent more and more of his time in his office, continuing to be both inaccessible and thoroughly enamored of his own greatness. He purchased two more plaques, one commemorating his prophecy and the other honoring him for capturing Crotch.

They were good for several trips on the Texas Ranger saddle. And the biblical scholars finally left town, having failed to trace Buck's life back any further than Tater, Oklahoma, locate any living relatives, or get an audience with Buck. Though a few journeyed to Tater, no Taterians personally remembered Buck or his family, and only two things could be confirmed by records: that he was born and that he was once the Tater All-Star Cotton-Picking Champion. Now, however, Buck was a hero *and* a prophet, and he was keeping it that way by keeping his mouth shut.

The canary lady bought a parakeet the day after she kissed Buck's boots. Then she fired her pimp and became a Christian Scientist, convinced that if God couldn't cure her illnesses, perhaps Buck could.

The Dorkas Rodd, a.k.a. Sloth, matter was finally disposed of. Axel wanted him to quietly plead guilty so that no one would ever know that he sired a dolt, and J.J. made arrangements for Dorkas to be sent to the new Reverse Punishment Crime Control Colony at Palm Springs. But Beatrice won out in the end. She hired the state's best criminal attorney, Giuseppi Fornasero, who did a masterful job. He put Dorkas on the stand, and five minutes later the judge ruled that he was an absolute idiot. After the idiocy hearing, all criminal charges were dropped, and Beatrice took him to Palestine, Illinois. There Axel's parents welcomed her and Dorkas with open arms and congratulated her for leaving their wicked, worthless son.

While the snows began to fly in the Sierras, the political climate began to heat up for the governor's race. The pros watched with anticipation, awaiting the day when Buck would come out with both guns blazing. But filing time came and passed, and Buck remained silent, inaccessible, and noncommittal. J.J. ran unopposed on the Democratic ticket; then, after the primary, he soundly thrashed his Republican opponent. When it was all over, Buck's stock was still on the rise. The people were now convinced that he was a true hero, a professional lawman, and a prophet with a direct line to God—not a politician after all.

Following his reelection, J.J. wasted no time in gearing up his presidential campaign. He began traveling around the country, delivering speeches, shaking hands, and finding time for several excursions to Alabama, where he became something of a hero. Before each trip, J.J. received hormone shots from his doctor, which got him through his sessions with Toni.

The presidential primaries were hectic, with J.J. and six Kennedys running in all of them. It was all quite boring until Amy Carter jumped in with the slogan "Don't Trust Me—Just Vote for Me." When she did, all hell broke loose in Congress over the fate of the James Earl Carter, Jr., Monument. There were fistfights in the halls, and death threats floated in the air like confetti. Amy took the hint and dropped out, but it was too late. Daddy's monument had been dynamited and the rubble dumped into the Potomac. Fearing retribution, the Republicans posted a twenty-four-hour guard around the Reagan Monument.

When the last of the bitterly contested primaries was over, no clear-cut winner had emerged, so the final decision had to be made in the smoke-filled rooms at the Democratic National Convention in Kansas City. There, when the lobbying, squabbling Kennedys effectively neutralized each other, J.J. became the Democratic nominee for the presidency of the United States.

At the close of the convention, after the last light was turned off, Red Ainess returned to their suite of rooms. J.J. and Axel, dressed in matching lavender tunics, were lounging on the floor.

181

Axel had a mouthful of pitted prunes, while J.J. savored a banana. They laughed and joked as they studied the White House floor plan laid out in front of them.

J.J. pointed to a cubicle next to the Oval Office. "Here's where your office will be, Red," he chirped.

Red, hands on hips, stared down at them. "It's a little early to be celebrating, isn't it, *guys?* That road to the White House is pretty long, pretty steep, and the polls are against us. I strongly suggest that you both get a good night's sleep. The real campaign starts bright and early tomorrow morning." With that, Red stomped off to his room.

J.J. and Axel turned toward each other, shrugged their shoulders in unison, and laughed. Then Axel grimaced as J.J. took a vicious bite off the end of the banana.

CHAPTER 23

THE REPUBLICAN kingmakers were ecstatic. Every poll taken at the close of the Democratic Convention indicated that any one of the top three of seven candidates running in the Republican primaries could beat J.J. by a comfortable margin. Like the Democratic primaries before them, however, the Republican primaries were indecisive. The Republicans would be going into a brokered convention, and the party leaders would proffer up the next president of the United States. "The Democrats have done it again," said a gleeful party functionary. "They gave us McGovern, Carter, and Mondale. And now they've served up Junior-Junior on a silver platter." The power brokers could hardly contain themselves when they met to decide on a candidate, three days before the convention. The smell of victory was intoxicating. But after several hours of heated debate, they remained deadlocked, unable to decide which one of the top three should be given the nomination. The meeting was in danger of falling into disarray.

Finally, with the help of two canes, an old man made his way to the front of the room. His long white hair stopped just short of his shoulders, and he wore an unkempt beard. His jowls hung far below his jawline. As he looked into the eyes of the kingmakers, one by one, the room fell silent.

"Gentlemen!" he said, with a resonance that projected authority and demanded respect. "Let me say this. You have the opportunity of a lifetime—the opportunity to once and for all *destroy* the Democratic party. You have at your fingertips the tool, or I should say the hammer, that you can use to *crush* the Democrats, to *beat* them into oblivion. This tool of which I speak, this hammer, this *sledgehammer*, is none other than Harry Hamilton Baal the Third." The kingmakers continued to stare up at him in disbelief. "To accomplish this annihilation, you must do everything in your power to ensure the election of J.J. Baal as president of the United States." Now they were sure of it: the old man was insane. The noise level began to elevate as one-on-one conversations spread across the room. "Gentlemen!" The booming voice brought the meeting back to order. "Let me say this about that. After four years of President J.J. Baal, the people of this great nation would *never* vote for a Democrat again. To assure this *victory*, you must nominate a loser. It's as simple as that."

As the idea permeated their minds, the kingmakers, one by one, rose to their feet. The applause was deafening as the old man made his way slowly across the room. When he reached the door, he turned to face the applauding crowd, and with all eyes on him, he managed to raise both arms and form victory signs with his fingers. Then his legs began to wobble. He dropped his arms, braced himself with the canes, and left. No one knew who he was, and in the excitement of the moment he was forgotten. Credit for his political masterstroke would be kept within the group. Later that night, the kingmakers decided who would not be king.

At the close of the Republican National Convention, the press gleefully buried the Republican party forevermore. And while the kingmakers celebrated their "victory," J.J. was busily writing his inaugural address.

Running under the slogan "The Man for All Reasons," J.J. swept the country, collecting the electoral votes of every state.

The Republican kingmakers threw themselves a victory party, and while they toasted the demise of the Democratic machine, J.J. delivered his election-night speech to a wild, cheering, supercharged crowd. When it was over, a picture flashed around the world: Harry Hamilton "J.J." Baal, president-elect of the United States, was flanked by his mother and father, with their hands joined high in the air and wide, toothy smiles on their faces. To the left of J.J.'s father, towering over the three of them, stood J.J.'s handpicked running mate—former Sheriff Buck Mullins, vice president-elect of the United States.

And behind them stood a group of their staunchest supporters and campaign workers, their arms stretched high in the air, their fingers forming victory signs: Red Ainess, Axel Rodd, Georgie and Toni Mandrocci, Hubert and his new wife, Wanda Flagella-Pickthorn-Henriksen, and Sheriff Buster Mullins, the second youngest man ever appointed to the office of Sheriff of Sacramento County, Sacramento, D.C.

And in San Diego, Penny Penny, Mrs. Horace Katt, watched it all on television while breast-feeding her two-month-old son, Horace Katt, Jr., a pleasant smile on her face.